Edgar Allan Poe · Daphne du Maurier
Shirley Jackson · Roald Dahl
Arthur C. Clarke

Famous Stories of Surprise

Model Interpretations

By Noreen O'Donovan

Ernst Klett Schulbuchverlag
Stuttgart Düsseldorf Berlin Leipzig

Lehrerbuch von Noreen O'Donovan, Pforzheim.
Beratende Mitarbeit: Professor Hans-Joachim Lechler, Fachleiter für Englisch am Seminar für Studienreferendare, Esslingen.

Acknowledgements

"The Lordly Ones" by Daphne du Maurier is reprinted by permission of Curtis Brown, London.

"The Lottery" by Shirley Jackson is reprinted by permission of Farrar, Straus & Giroux, Inc., New York.

"The Landlady" by Roald Dahl is reprinted from *Kiss Kiss* (1959) by permission of Mohrbooks, Zürich. The story originally appeared in *The New Yorker*.

"History Lesson" by Arthur C. Clarke is reprinted by permission of Peter & Paul Fritz AG, Zürich.

Pictures: dpa, Frankfurt: p. 13; David Higham Associates, London: p. 95; Lawrence Jackson Hyman: p. 58; Ullstein-Camera Press Ltd., Berlin: pp. 38, 78.

> The stories to which these interpretations refer are also available in a students' edition: *Famous Stories of Surprise* (Klettnummer 5776)
>
> The cassette accompanying this book contains the stories by Edgar Allan Poe, Shirley Jackson, Roald Dahl and Arthur C. Clarke (Klettnummer 57762).

1. Auflage   1   5   4   3   2 | 97   96   95   94

Alle Drucke dieser Auflage können im Unterricht nebeneinander benutzt werden, sie sind untereinander unverändert. Die letzte Zahl bezeichnet das Jahr dieses Druckes.
© dieser Ausgabe Ernst Klett Schulbuchverlag GmbH, Stuttgart 1988.
Alle Rechte für diese Ausgabe vorbehalten.
Umschlaggestaltung: Hans Lämmle, Stuttgart.
Druck: Gutmann+Co., 74388 Talheim. Printed in Germany.
ISBN 3-12-577610-4

Contents

Introduction 4

A Note to Teachers 5

Edgar Allan Poe, The Cask of Amontillado 7
Biographical Notes 13

Background, Content and Analysis 17
Teaching Notes 21

Daphne du Maurier, The Lordly Ones 25
Biographical Notes 38

Background, Content and Analysis 42
Teaching Notes 44

Shirley Jackson, The Lottery 50
Biographical Notes 58

Background, Content and Analysis 60
Teaching Notes 64

Roald Dahl, The Landlady 70
Biographical Notes 78

Background, Content and Analysis 81
Teaching Notes 82

Arthur C. Clarke, History Lesson 87
Biographical Notes 95

Background, Content and Analysis 99
Teaching Notes 102

Introduction

All good storytellers play with their readers' expectations. (Or with their listeners' or viewers' expectations, for that matter – but we are concerned here with the written word.)

Many of these expectations exist prior to the reading of the story. There are certain conventions as to literary form and content that readers will be familiar with and expect the storyteller to conform to. Other expectations are generated as the story proceeds, but even these will be influenced by the readers' previous experience of both life and literature.

The storyteller then has the option of fulfilling or confounding these expectations. At one end of the scale lies reassurance, but also the danger of boredom. Why read on, if the story-line is so familiar that you can predict the outcome? At the other end of the scale lies the danger of confusion and frustration. A writer who completely disregards the rules and conventions of storytelling will fail to communicate with his or her readers.

No story can therefore function without some degree of suspense – which can be defined as the uncertainty generated in the reader's mind as to whether an expectation will be fulfilled or confounded, and, if the latter, in what way.

The stories in this collection have been chosen for the high degree of suspense they offer. Their suspense can, however, consist of a lulling of sensibilities prior to an unexpected ending. It might, therefore, be better to refer to the quality they share as an "S"-factor: suspense, surprise, shock.

Each of these stories features some kind of "twist in the tail", which can be anything from shocking to humorous. A common criticism of such stories is that they can only be read once. This is not necessarily true. Even when the ending is known, there is considerable pleasure in discovering how the effect is achieved, how the author has managed to "lead you up the garden path". And it may take several readings of some of these stories to fully appreciate the significance of the ending.

Be that as it may, no reader should be deprived of the chance of being pleasurably startled the first time round. For that reason, the less said here about the individual stories the better.

A Note to Teachers

How do you teach a short story with a surprise ending? Or any story of suspense for that matter?

It might be easier to say how not to do it. One common approach is to tell the students to read the whole story at home before starting to discuss it in class. Teachers who favour this approach may have Poe's famous dictum in mind about the "unique or single effect"[1] which every good short story should achieve, and want nothing to come between their students and this "effect". An admirable aim, indeed, but not so easy to achieve – especially with a foreign language class.

At best – using this approach – the story will have the intended effect on the more advanced students, and they will remember enough to be able to talk about it later in class. But what about those students who stumble over some trivial language difficulty, and thus miss some point essential (let's say) to the build-up of tension? They will struggle on through the story, read the outcome, but its effect will be lost on them. They will have been cheated of one of the elementary pleasures of fiction. And no amount of subsequent explication can make up for that.

The "unique or single effect" of a story is, after all, quite different from that of a picture on the wall. By its very nature it unfolds in time, and is the cumulative product of processes triggered off in the mind of the reader at each stage in the story by the art of the storyteller.

For this reason, the teaching strategies recommended in this book are all variations of the step-by-step approach. Very often we recommend that some – or all – of the reading be done in class, or that part of a story be presented through the medium of the recording. In this way the teacher accompanies the students as they get to know the characters and the situation, speculate on the possible outcome and gradually discover where the author is leading them. This "first reading" stage should not, of course, be dragged out longer than is necessary, or any suspense generated will be lost.

Do not worry if such a step-by-step approach should prove too slow for some students. Those who insist on skipping ahead, or reading more than is required of them will, by and large, be the experienced readers who are well able to take care of themselves. And a discrepancy within the class between those who have read to the end and those who haven't need not be a bad thing. As long as the speed-readers do not insist on spoiling everyone else's fun, the difference can even be exploited for added interest.

---

[1] From Poe's review of Hawthorne's *Twice Told Tales* (1842).

It must be stressed here that our Teaching Notes are meant as suggestions, and not as an attempt to lay down the law for the teacher. No two classes are identical, no two students are identical. It is therefore impossible to anticipate all the reader's reactions at all stages of a story. For this reason we have largely avoided giving model answers to the suggested questions, and instead merely indicated the range of possible responses. But this flexibility may not be enough. Teachers must be prepared in many cases to adapt the unit structure mapped out here to suit the needs of their classes and their timetables, to work out a different strategy if necessary with the help of the information given in the Background, Content and Analysis section. Most important of all, they should be flexible enough to change course if their students' responses call for it.

Teachers should also decide for themselves which stories should be read when. The given sequence represents a comprise between chronology and balance in setting and theme, but has the disadvantage of placing the most difficult story (Poe) at the beginning. For less advanced classes it might be more adviseable for example, to start with the easier Dahl story, and either omit Poe or leave his story to the end. The other three stories are of moderate difficulty.

Though primarily intended as aids to understanding the stories, the Annotations are set up so that they can, if desired, be used for vocabulary-learning purposes. The words given in bold print are those which (we suggest) ought to be learned at this stage of language learning.

Edgar Allan Poe

The Cask of Amontillado

The thousand injuries of Fortunato I had borne as I best could; but when he ventured upon insult, I vowed revenge. You, who so well know the nature of my soul, will not suppose, however, that I gave utterance to a threat. *At length* I would be avenged; this was a point definitively settled – but the very definitiveness with which it was resolved, precluded the idea of risk. I must not only punish, but punish with impunity. A wrong is unredressed when retribution overtakes its redresser. It is equally unredressed when the avenger fails to make himself felt as such to him who has done the wrong.

It must be understood, that neither by word nor deed had I given Fortunato cause to doubt my good-will. I continued, as was my wont, to smile in his face, and he did not perceive that my smile *now* was at the thought of his immolation.

He had a weak point – this Fortunato – although in other regards he was a man to be respected and even feared. He prided himself on his connoisseurship in wine. Few Italians have the true virtuoso spirit. For the most part their enthusiasm is adopted to suit the time and opportunity – to practise imposture upon the British and Austrian *millionaires*. In painting and gemmary Fortunato, like his countrymen, was a quack – but in the matter of old wines he was sincere. In this respect I did not differ from him materially: I was skilful in the Italian vintages myself, and bought largely whenever I could.

It was about dusk, one evening during the supreme madness of the carnival season, that I encountered my friend. He accosted me with excessive warmth, for he had been drinking much. The man wore motley. He had on a tight-fitting parti-striped dress, and his head was surmounted by the conical cap and bells. I was so pleased to see him, that I thought I should never have done wringing his hand.

I said to him: "My dear Fortunato, you are luckily met. How remarkably well you are looking to-day! But I have received a pipe of what passes for Amontillado, and I have my doubts."

"How?" said he. "Amontillado? A pipe? Impossible! And in the middle of the carnival!"

"I have my doubts," I replied; "and I was silly enough to pay the full

Amontillado price without consulting you in the matter. You were not to be found, and I was fearful of losing a bargain."

"Amontillado!"

"I have my doubts."

"Amontillado!"

"And I must satisfy them."

"Amontillado!"

"As you are engaged, I am on my way to Luchesi. If any one has a critical turn, it is he. He will tell me —"

"Luchesi cannot tell Amontillado from Sherry."

"And yet some fools will have it that his taste is a match for your own."

"Come, let us go."

"Whither?"

"To your vaults."

"My friend, no; I will not impose upon your good nature. I perceive you have an engagement. Luchesi —"

"I have no engagement; – come."

"My friend, no. It is not the engagement, but the severe cold with which I perceive you are afflicted. The vaults are insufferably damp. They are encrusted with nitre."

"Let us go, nevertheless. The cold is merely nothing. Amontillado! You have been imposed upon. And as for Luchesi, he cannot distinguish Sherry from Amontillado."

Thus speaking, Fortunato possessed himself of my arm. Putting on a mask of black silk, and drawing a *roquelaire* closely about my person, I suffered him to hurry me to my palazzo.

There were no attendants at home; they had absconded to make merry in honor of the time. I had told them that I should not return until the morning, and had given them explicit orders not to stir from the house. These orders were sufficient, I well knew, to insure their immediate disappearance, one and all, as soon as my back was turned.

I took from their sconces two flambeaux, and giving one to Fortunato, bowed him through several suites of rooms to the archway that led into the vaults. I passed down a long and winding staircase, requesting him to be cautious as he followed. We came at length to the foot of the descent, and stood together on the damp ground of the catacombs of the Montresors.

The gait of my friend was unsteady, and the bells upon his cap jingled as he strode.

"The pipe?" said he.

"It is farther on," said I; "but observe the white web-work which gleams from these cavern walls."

He turned toward me, and looked into my eyes with two filmy orbs that distilled the rheum of intoxication.

"Nitre?" he asked, at length.

"Nitre," I replied. "How long have you had that cough?"

"Ugh! ugh! ugh! – ugh! ugh! ugh! – ugh! ugh! ugh! – ugh! ugh! ugh! – ugh! ugh! ugh!"

My poor friend found it impossible to reply for many minutes.

"It is nothing," he said at last.

"Come," I said, with decision, "we will go back; your health is precious. You are rich, respected, admired, beloved; you are happy, as once I was. You are a man to be missed. For me it is no matter. We will go back; you will be ill, and I cannot be responsible. Besides, there is Luchesi —"

"Enough," he said; "the cough is a mere nothing; it will not kill me. I shall not die of a cough."

"True – true," I replied; "and, indeed, I had no intention of alarming you unnecessarily; but you should use all proper caution. A draught of this Medoc will defend us from the damps."

Here I knocked off the neck of a bottle which I drew from a long row of its fellows that lay upon the mould.

"Drink," I said, presenting him the wine.

He raised it to his lips with a leer. He paused and nodded to me familiarly, while his bells jingled.

"I drink," he said, "to the buried that repose around us."

"And I to your long life."

He again took my arm, and we proceeded.

"These vaults," he said, "are extensive."

"The Montresors," I replied, "were a great and numerous family."

"I forget your arms."

"A huge human foot d'or, in a field azure; the foot crushes a serpent rampant whose fangs are imbedded in the heel."

"And the motto?"

"Nemo me impune lacessit."

"Good!" he said.

The wine sparkled in his eyes and the bells jingled. My own fancy grew warm with the Medoc. We had passed through walls of piled bones, with casks and puncheons intermingling, into the inmost recesses of the catacombs. I paused again, and this time I made bold to seize Fortunato by an arm above the elbow.

"The nitre!" I said; "see, it increases. It hangs like moss upon the vaults. We are below the river's bed. The drops of moisture trickle among the bones. Come, we will go back ere it is too late. Your cough —"

"It is nothing," he said; "let us go on. But first, another draught of the Medoc."

I broke and reached him a flagon of De Grâve. He emptied it at a breath. His eyes flashed with a fierce light. He laughed and threw the bottle upward with a gesticulation I did not understand.

I looked at him in surprise. He repeated the movement – a grotesque one.

"You do not comprehend?" he said.

"Not I," I replied.

"Then you are not of the brotherhood."

"How?"

"You are not of the masons."

"Yes, yes," I said; "yes, yes."

"You? Impossible! A mason?"

"A mason," I replied.

"A sign," he said.

"It is this," I answered, producing a trowel from beneath the folds, of my *roquelaire*.

"You jest," he exclaimed, recoiling a few paces. "But let us proceed to the Amontillado."

"Be it so," I said, replacing the tool beneath the cloak, and again offering him my arm. He leaned upon it heavily. We continued our route in search of the Amontillado. We passed through a range of low arches, descended, passed on, and descending again, arrived at a deep crypt, in which the foulness of the air caused our flambeaux rather to glow than flame.

At the most remote end of the crypt there appeared another less spacious. Its walls had been lined with human remains, piled to the vault overhead, in the fashion of the great catacombs of Paris. Three sides of this interior crypt were still ornamented in this manner. From the fourth the bones had been thrown down, and lay promiscuously upon the earth, forming at one point a mound of some size. Within the wall thus exposed by the displacing of the bones, we perceived a still interior recess, in depth about four feet, in width three, in height six or seven. It seemed to have been constructed for no especial use within itself, but formed merely the interval between two of the colossal supports of the roof of the catacombs, and was backed by one of their circumscribing walls of solid granite.

It was in vain that Fortunato, uplifting his dull torch, endeavored to pry into the depth of the recess. Its termination the feeble light did not enable us to see.

"Proceed," I said; "herein is the Amontillado. As for Luchesi —"

"He is an ignoramus," interrupted my friend, as he stepped unsteadily forward, while I followed immediately at his heels. In an instant he had reached the extremity of the niche, and finding his progress arrested by the rock, stood stupidly bewildered. A moment more and I had fettered him to the granite. In its surface were two iron staples, distant from each other about two feet, horizontally. From one of these depended a short chain, from the other a padlock. Throwing the links about his waist, it was but the work of a few seconds to secure it. He was too much astounded to resist. Withdrawing the key I stepped back from the recess.

"Pass your hand," I said, "over the wall; you cannot help feeling the nitre. Indeed it is *very* damp. Once more let me *implore* you to return. No? Then I must positively leave you. But I must first render you all the little attentions in my power."

"The Amontillado!" ejaculated my friend, not yet recovered from his astonishment.

"True," I replied; "the Amontillado."

As I said these words I busied myself among the pile of bones of which I have before spoken. Throwing them aside, I soon uncovered a quantity of building stone and mortar. With these materials and with the aid of my trowel, I began vigorously to wall up the entrance of the niche.

I had scarcely laid the first tier of the masonry when I discovered that the intoxication of Fortunato had in a great measure worn off. The earliest indication I had of this was a low moaning cry from the depth of the recess. It was *not* the cry of a drunken man. There was then a long and obstinate silence. I laid the second tier, and the third, and the fourth; and then I heard the furious vibrations of the chain. The noise lasted for several minutes, during which, that I might hearken to it with the more satisfaction, I ceased my labors and sat down upon the bones. When at last the clanking subsided, I resumed the trowel, and finished without interruption the fifth, the sixth, and the seventh tier. The wall was now nearly upon a level with my breast. I again paused, and holding the flambeaux over the mason-work, threw a few feeble rays upon the figure within.

A succession of loud and shrill screams, bursting suddenly from the throat of the chained form, seemed to thrust me violently back. For a brief moment I hesitated – I trembled. Unsheathing my rapier, I began to grope with it about the recess; but the thought of an instant reassured me. I placed my hand upon the solid fabric of the catacombs, and felt satisfied. I reapproached the wall. I replied to the yells of him who clamored. I re-echoed – I aided – I surpassed them in volume and in strength. I did this, and the clamorer grew still.

It was now midnight, and my task was drawing to a close. I had completed the eighth, the ninth, and the tenth tier. I had finished a portion of the last and the eleventh; there remained but a single stone to be fitted and plastered in. I struggled with its weight; I placed it partially in its destined position. But now there came from out the niche a low laugh that erected the hairs upon my head. It was succeeded by a sad voice, which I had difficulty in recognizing as that of the noble Fortunato. The voice said —

"Ha! ha! ha! – he! he! – a very good joke indeed – an excellent jest. We will have many a rich laugh about it at the palazzo – he! he! he! – over our wine – he! he! he!"

"The Amontillado!" I said.

"He! he! he! – he! he! he! – yes, the Amontillado. But is it not getting late? Will not they be awaiting us at the palazzo, the Lady Fortunato and the rest? Let us be gone."

"Yes," I said, "let us be gone."

"For the love of God, Montresor!"

"Yes," I said, "for the love of God!"

But to these words I hearkened in vain for a reply. I grew impatient. I called aloud:

"Fortunato!"

No answer. I called again:

"Fortunato!"

No answer still. I thrust a torch through the remaining aperture and let it fall within. There came forth in return only a jingling of the bells. My heart grew sick – on account of the dampness of the catacombs. I hastened to make an end of my labor. I forced the last stone into its position; I plastered it up. Against the new masonry I re-erected the old rampart of bones. For the half of a century no mortal has disturbed them. *In pace requiescat!*

Biographical Notes

Edgar Allan Poe is widely considered the father of the psychological horror tale, and of the modern detective story.

He was born in Boston in 1809, the second child of David and Elizabeth Poe, both of whom were actors. His parents died soon after his birth, and he was taken as a foster-child by John and Frances Allan (hence Poe's middle name), of Richmond, Virginia. He went to school there and in England, where the family lived for five years.

He began writing poems at an early age, the first volume being published during his one term at the University of Virginia in 1826. He had to leave when – after a family quarrel – his foster-father refused to pay his fees and other debts. Around the same time he suffered a brain lesion which gave rise to recurrent periods of mental illness. After two years in the army he briefly attended West Point military academy, but he was discontented and contrived to be expelled. In the following years he held a series of jobs as editor of literary magazines in New York, Philadelphia and elsewhere, and published numerous short stories, poems and reviews.

After his young wife died of tuberculosis in 1847, his own health deteriorated. In 1849 he was found in delirium in a Baltimore tavern and died soon after.

"The Cask of Amontillado" (published 1846) ist one of his best-known stories, and shows him to be a master of atmosphere and suspense. Others include "The Murders in the Rue Morgue", "The Tell-Tale Heart" and "The Fall of the House of Usher".

Annotations

5		cask	barrel, large container
		Amontillado	a kind of sherry
	2	to venture upon	to dare, to go so far as
		to vow [vaʊ]	to promise solemnly
	3	to give utterance to	to express
	4	to be avenged	to have revenge
	5	to preclude	to rule out
	6	with impunity [ɪmˈpjuːnɪtɪ]	with no danger of being punished
		to redress	to set right; *here:* to revenge
	7	retribution	punishment
	10	my wont [əʊ]	my usual custom
	12	immolation	sacrificial killing
	14	connoisseurship	expert judgement
	15	virtuoso	*here:* a connoisseur of the arts
	17	imposture	deception
	18	gemmary [ˈdʒ---]	the study or knowledge of precious stones
		quack	person who pretends to be an expert
	20	vintage [ˈvɪntɪdʒ]	the wine of a particular year
	22	**dusk**	time just after sunset
	23	to accost	to approach, to greet
	24	motley	multi-coloured costume
	25	conical [ˈkɒn--]	cone-shaped
	26	to have done (wringing…)	to be finished
	27	to wring	*here:* to shake (hands)

	29 pipe	*here:* cask
	to pass for	to be accepted as
6	6 satisfy them	find out if their (doubts) are justified
	8 to have a critical turn	to be critical or discerning
	13 whither?	*(arch.)* where?
	14 vault	underground chamber with an arched roof
	15 to impose upon	to take advantage of
	19 to be afflicted with	to suffer from
	damp	moist, not dry
	20 nitre	potassium nitrate, a white salt
	24 to possess o.s. of	to take hold of
	25 roquelaire *(French)*	a cloak reaching to the knees
	to suffer s.o. to	to allow s.o. to
	27 to abscond	to run away
	29 to stir	*here:* to move
	32 sconce	a holder fixed to the wall
	flambeaux *(French)*	flaming torches
	33 archway	rounded stone entrance
	38 **gait**	walk, way of walking
7	1 web-work	s.th. which resembles the web of a spider
	3 orb	globe, ball; *here:* eyes
	filmy	covered with a film, hazy
	4 to distill the rheum of [ruːm]	*here:* to concentrate the effects of
	intoxication	drunkenness
	18 draught [drɑːft]	drink
	21 its fellows	its "comrades", i.e. the other bottles
	mould [əʊ]	fungus growth caused by damp
	23 leer	a lustful look
	25 **to repose**	to rest
	30 arms	*here:* family's coat of arms
	31 d'or	(in heraldry) of gold
	azure ['eɪʒjʊə]	(in heraldry) blue
	serpent ['--]	snake
	32 rampant ['--]	(in heraldry) standing up
	fang	poison tooth
	34 Nemo me impune lacessit *(Latin)*	no one attacks me with impunity
	38 puncheon ['pʌntʃən]	cask, barrel
	inmost recess	part of the cavern furthest in
	39 to make bold to	to venture, to dare
8	3 ere [eə]	*(arch.)* before
	6 flagon ['flægən]	large bottle
	15 **mason** ['meɪsn]	*here:* freemason; *otherwise:* person who builds walls
	20 trowel [aʊ]	tool for spreading plaster or mortar
	22 **to jest**	to joke
	to recoil	to move back in shock
	pace	step
	27 crypt	underground chamber
	29 **remote**	far away

		Poe, *The Cask of Amontillado*	
	33	promiscuous [–'– – –]	*here:* mixed up all together
	34	mound	heap, pile
	38	colossal supports	thick pillars
	39	circumscribing	surrounding
	40	to pry	to look closely
9	1	termination	end
		feeble	weak
	4	ignoramus [– –'eɪ–]	ignorant person
	7	**bewildered** [ɪ]	puzzled, confused
		to fetter	to chain
	8	staples	U-shaped holders
	9	to depend	*here (arch.):* to hang
	10	**padlock**	lock which can be attached to a chain or staple
	15	to render … attentions	to perform services, to do s.o. favours
	24	tier [ɪə]	layer
	26	**to moan**	to make a sound as if in pain
	27	**obstinate** ['ɒbstɪnɪt]	stubborn, not wishing to capitulate
	30	to hearken ['hɑːkən]	to listen
	31	clanking	sound made by chains
		to subside	to stop
	32	**to resume**	to start s.th. again
	36	**succession**	series
	38	to unsheath a rapier ['reɪpjə]	to pull out a long, thin sword
		to grope	to feel around in the dark
10	1	to clamor [æ]	to make a lot of noise, to yell
	2	**to surpass**	to be better, louder, etc.
	7	destined ['destɪnd]	planned, predetermined
	21	**in vain**	without success
	26	aperture ['æp– –]	opening
	30	rampart ['– –]	protective or defensive wall
	31	mortal	*here:* human being
		In pace requiescat *(Latin)*	may he rest in peace

Interpretation and Teaching Notes

Background, Content and Analysis

"There are certain themes of which the interest is all-absorbing, but which are too entirely horrible for the purposes of legitimate fiction ... To be buried alive is, beyond question, the most terrific of these extremes which has ever fallen to the lot of mere humanity."[1]

Thus the narrator of Poe's "The Premature Burial", who claims to be a reporter of documentary truth and not a writer of fiction. This device allows Poe to deal with a theme he has been obsessed with all his life. It comes up again and again in his writings: in "The Fall of the House of Usher", in "Berenice", in "Ligeia"; it is used with probably the greatest effect in "The Cask of Amontillado". It seems that the very horribleness of the theme that served Poe as the ideal vehicle for his imagination.

In the case of "The Cask", the theme of being buried alive does, however, appear to have some basis in fact. During Poe's short spell in the army (1927-29) he was stationed for a while at Fort Independence, Boston, where (it is said)[2] he heard of a murder that had taken place at the fort ten years earlier. To avenge the death of a popular young lieutenant in a duel, his friends had got the officer who had killed him drunk, taken him to the deepest dungeon in the fort, chained him to the floor of a niche, and walled it up, leaving him to die.

This story was corroborated in 1905 – long after Poe's death – when workmen renovating the fort knocked down a wall and found a skeleton in what remained of an 1812 army uniform. So Poe may very well have heard such rumours in 1827. If so, it stayed in his mind long enough to be used in a story published twenty years later.

For Poe the theme of being buried alive represents the ultimate horror – and the ultimate revenge. Horror, revenge, guilt, an exotic setting, a gothic atmosphere, almost unbearable suspense – all these elements present in "The Cask" combine to make it one of Poe's most typical spine-chillers.

The artificial elements of the story may well have been added to make it conform to the conventions of the gothic horror tale. In any case, their

---

[1] Edgar Allan Poe, "The Premature Burial", 1844.
[2] *The United States in Literature* (Glenview, Ill.: Scott, Foresman & Co. 1985) quotes a publication called *Mysterious New England* (© 1974, Yankee Inc.) as a source. Thomas Oliver Mabott, editor of *The Collected Works of Edgar Allan Poe* (Harvard University Press, 1978) mentions a number of other tales and factual reports which may have suggested the idea to Poe.

immediate effect (especially the effect of the exotic setting) is to remove the happenings described away from the realm of everyday reality and into a realm – no, not of fantasy, but one sufficiently far removed from the readers' familiar surroundings to overcome any resistance on their part to the extremes of the human mind[3].

It is obvious from the beginning of the story that it takes place in a Mediterranean country, most probably Italy. This impression is confirmed as the story progresses, through references to the carnival (**5** 22–26) and the names of the noblemen involved. That they are noblemen is strongly suggested by the haughty bearing of the narrator and the importance given to connoisseurship in wine (**6** 1ff). One might get the impression that the time is the late middle ages, were it not for the reference to "British and Austrian millionnaires" (**5** 17), which places it clearly in the mid-nineteenth century, i.e.the present, for Poe and his immediate readers.

Also obvious from the start is that the story is being told long after it has happened, and not directly to the reader, but to somebody close to the narrator (**5** 2–3)[4]. It is as if we are eavesdropping on a confession of some sort, of which we have missed the greater part[5].

Thus Poe sets the seeds of suspense. We are left in the dark[6] about the "thousand injuries of Fortunato" (**5** 1), but have no reason to doubt the Narrator's certainty that he "would be avenged" (**5** 4). What he reveals of his character lends credence to his threat, especially the pride and arrogance expressed by his remarks about the failings of the Italians (**5** 15) – his own name, Montresor, suggests that he is at least part French, or of French descent.

The unfortunate Fortunato could not be more ill-matched: slightly drunk, rather ridiculous in his carnival motley, and totally oblivious to Montresor's evil intent. From the initial encounter onwards, suspense intensifies, as do the ironies of the situation. In fact, irony is an integral element in the

---

[3] Cf. Niel Hoffman, *Poe, Poe, Poe,* Doubleday, New York 1972; esp. "Preface", p.ix.: "Although the characters in his tales are without exception fantastic personages, they must touch some deep, responsive nerve hidden in ourselves. Whose image do we see in Poe's insane criminals ...? ... Of whose experiences has he the power to remind us?"

[4] The identity of this person is a matter for speculation. Cf. John Hagopian and Martin Dolch, "The Cask of Amontillado" in *Insight I – Analyses of American Literature,* Hirschgraben, Frankfurt/Main 1962 (p.206).

[5] It has been maintained that this story has "an end, but no beginning or middle", i.e. that it is "all denouement". John Gardner, *The Art of Fiction,* Knopf, New York 1983 (pp.47, 133).

[6] Hagopian (op. cit., p.204) includes a number of speculations on this matter. He tends to take Montresor seriously as the injured party, quoting as evidence Fortunato's tactless remarks (family arms, freemasons).

suspense. We share to an extent Montresor's ironic amusement at the way Fortunato rises to the bait, in the form of a challenge to his connoisseurship in wine (**6** 10–26). But we do not yet know whether the joke will not be at our expense.

Only gradually does the nature of the macabre joke dawn on the reader, again through a series of ironic exchanges which Montresor, no doubt, enjoys immensely. He "will not die of a cough", Fortunato protests, now determined to enter the trap. To which Montresor replies, "True, true." What Montresor intends him to die of is indicated with almost brazen openess when he produces a trowel, claiming – to Fortunato's puzzlement – to be a "mason" (**8** 15–21).

The victim's failure to understand his predicament may be a source of malicious amusement to Montresor, confirming his contempt for this leering, drunken fool. But the irony is double-edged, as will emerge with full force at the end of the story.

One exchange is particularly significant. In the course of some seemingly trivial conversation on their way through the catacombs, Fortunato asks about the Montresor family's arms, which he has forgotten (**7** 30). (One wonders at this point whether all the insults and injuries Montresor thinks him guilty of are of such a trivial nature.) When they are described to him, he fails to notice the implicit threat, and merely admires the rightness of the motto, "Nobody insults me with impunity."

The alert reader will here be reminded of Montresor's remarks at the beginning of the story about the necessary conditions for successful revenge (**5** 5–8), namely to punish with impunity, and "to make himself felt" as avenger. Is he making himself felt as such?

In the meantime, the suspense intensifies. An atmosphere of terror is invoked as the two men progress through the nitre-encrusted vaults, lined with human remains and lit only by their flickering torches. Our worst expectations are confirmed when the victim is finally clapped in irons (**9** 10–12). But even then we resist the obvious conclusion. It may after all be a macabre joke, and maybe even a madman can be forced to relent.

But there is no relenting. As Montresor proceeds in workmanlike fashion to wall up the niche, Fortunato's intoxication begins to wear off. He begins to realize that Montresor is deadly serious. His "low moaning cry" (**9** 26) brings Montresor some of the satisfaction he had been hoping for, but a series of screams causes him to hesitate (**9** 36–38). Once again a build-up of suspense: is he going to relent after all? No, he is only worried about whether the chains will hold. He continues his work and, ignoring Fortunato's final plea, plasters in the final stone.

Has Montresor, after all, achieved the perfect revenge he had planned? There is room for doubt. "My heart grew sick," he tells us (**10** 27–28), on hearing nothing but a jingling of bells in response to his call. The reason he hastens to add is a bit too glib to be convincing. But what is the real reason?

Is it remorse for what he has done? If so, it is quickly suppressed. Even if he is, as some critics have concluded[7], telling the story to a priest, possibly on his death-bed, then it is what Catholics call a "bad confession", and he must expect to face eternal damnation[8].

Another possibility is that he realizes at that moment that his own conditions for perfect revenge have not been fulfilled. Although Fortunato had sobered up sufficiently to recognize his predicament, there are no signs that he recognized his tormentor as an avenger. Indeed, he seems to have no awareness whatsoever of having insulted or injured Montresor in any way. His final plea (**10** 11–17), in which he pathetically pretends to see the whole horrifying affair as a joke, shows that he sees him as a madman who can at best be "jollied out of a senseless act"[9].

This ambiguity can be seen as a fault in the story[10]. But the main point remains clear. Either way, the threat implicit in the Montresor family arms has been fully borne out – in a way the avenger had not even considered. For him, no doubt, the serpent's fangs imbedded in the heel of the avenger's foot (**7** 31–32) represented the "thousand injuries of Fortunato". But it makes a lot more sense to see them as the victim's posthumous revenge on the failed avenger[11].

So who is the victor, and who is the victim? No discussion of this question will fail to take note of the similarities between the two men. They are both noblemen – even the narrator acknowledges in passing his adversary's nobility (**10** 10). They have similar interests, and share a similar failing – pride. Even their names are similar: Montresor, Fortunato. Their differences, where they exist, are complementary, like two sides of the same coin[12].

Without going to the extremes of some Freudian analysts[13], it is difficult to deny that in some sense, Montresor is bent on taking revenge on an aspect of his own personality. And in carrying out his threat, he has effec-

---

[7] Cf. Hagopian (op. cit., p. 206).

[8] Cf. James F. Cooney, "'The Cask of Amontillado': Some Further Ironies" in *Studies in Short Fiction* 11, 1974 (pp. 195–196).

[9] Hagopian op. cit. (p. 205).

[10] Hagopian op. cit. (p. 205).

[11] Cf. Kathryn Montgomery Harris, "Ironic Revenge in Poe's 'The Cask of Amontillado'" in *Studies in Short Fiction* 6, 1969 (p. 334). For an alternative interpretation of the significance of the family arms cf. Walter Stepp, "The Ironic Double in Poe's 'The Cask of Amontillado'" in *Studies in Short Fiction 13,* 1976 (p. 44).

[12] The point is further elaborated by Hoffman (op. cit., pp. 211–212, 223–226) and Stepp (op. cit., pp. 447–449).

[13] Cf. Dr. Marie Bonaparte, *The Life and Works of Edgar Allan Poe, A Psychoanalytic Interpretation,* Atlantic Highlands, New Jersey: Humanities Press 1971.

tively walled himself up in the dungeons of his revenge. For the rest of his life, this one act will dominate his consciousness. Seen this way, it hardly matters who is actually referred to in the final wish: May he rest in peace.

It remains to be considered in what sense "The Cask of Amontillado" is a story of surprise. Indeed, its inclusion as the first story in an anthology of this title might have encouraged readers to hope for (or even to expect) some twist at the end to prevent Montresor carrying out his threats. If so, this has merely strengthened an element already present in the narrative – its suspense. And let this be a lesson to any readers who think they know what to expect from a story of surprise!

Recommended Teaching Units (Overview)

I. Classroom presentation of first third of story, to **6** 26 (exposition, introduction of both characters, theme of planned revenge).

II. After home preparation, discussion of content up to **9** 19 (progress through catacombs to point where Fortunato is chained), atmosphere, irony, suspense.

III. After home preparation, discussion of effect and meaning of ending.

Unit I
The Threat

Note: No special preparation is necessary, since, with the aid of the recording, a first reading of this section can easily be accomplished in one lesson period, leaving enough time for comprehension questions and discussion of the relevant points. Teachers to whom the recording is not available or who prefer intensive (as opposed to cursory) reading right from the start, may of course set the reading of this section as homework in advance.

1. The exposition (**5** 1–21, first reading) Ideally, the recording should be used here (about 2 minutes playing time), with books either closed or open at text or vocabulary – depending on the needs of the class and the teacher's preference. Alternatively, the teacher could read these introductory paragraphs to the class, or allow them to be read silently.

2. Comprehension questions
Who is speaking?
Who is he speaking to?
Who is he talking about?
What is the speaker's attitude to this person?
What exactly has this person done to the speaker/narrator?
What does the speaker/narrator want to do?
What is the setting of the story? What country? What period?

Regardless of how well some students are able to answer these questions, the class should be given the opportunity to listen to the recording a second time, to correct or augment their first impressions or to look up words they don't know (e.g. in the difficult passage **5** 4–8, which may require translation or paraphrase).

Note that only vague or tentative answers can be given to many of the above questions at this stage *(Who is speaking? What does he want ...?)*, and some will remain matters for speculation to the end *(Who ... to? What exactly ...?)*. The main object here is to ensure that the students get into the story quickly, and that their appetites are whetted for such information as the author will supply as the story proceeds.

3. The encounter (first reading, **5** 22–**6** 26)
Any of the procedures mentioned under point 1. may be chosen. Playing time of the recording: roughly 3 minutes.

4. Fortunato (comprehension questions)
What has the narrator already told us about Fortunato before this encounter?
It should be noted that Fortunato's strong point (connoisseurship) is closely linked with his "weak point" (**5** 13), pride.
How much of this is confirmed in the passage describing the encounter?
How is he dressed? Why?

5. The threat (comprehension, speculation)
How does the narrator behave towards Fortunato when they meet?
Is he sincere in what he says? What makes you think so?
What do you think he really has in mind?
If necessary, the students should be reminded of or allowed to re-read the narrator's introductory remarks (exposition) before indulging in any speculation as to his intentions toward Fortunato.

Homework: Read to **9** 19 (from the beginning if only the recording has been used up to here).

Unit II
Atmosphere, Irony and Suspense

1. Comprehension
The students should be asked for a short summary of the action up to 9 19 –
i. e. the point where Fortunato is clapped in irons.

2. Atmosphere and suspense
Did you know beforehand that this is what would happen?
Why?/Why not?
What was your reaction when it did happen?
Individual answers called for here. Those who claim to have expected, feared or even known what the narrator would do will have been influenced not only by his introductory remarks but by the gothic atmosphere conjured up by the description of the surroundings. The most relevant or striking passages should be quoted.

3. Irony and suspense
How does Fortunato's appearance and behaviour contribute to the suspense?
Did you find yourself laughing at him for cutting such a ridiculous figure and being so blind to his predicament – or sympathizing with him and hoping he would escape?
Again, individual reactions called for. Most students will have to admit to a certain enjoyment of Montresor's maliciously ironic remarks about his guest's health, etc. while being shocked at their implications. The most striking passages should be quoted, and the relevance of the first-person point of view touched upon.

4. Montresor
What have you learned in the meantime about the narrator?
What do you still not know about him – and would like to know?
Already revealed: his name, his family pride, his malicious sense of humour, his hatred of Fortunato and desire for revenge. Still unexplained: revenge for what? The students may be encouraged to speculate and look for clues in the story so far:
Do you think Fortunato's offence is something serious or trivial?
Is Montresor mad?
Will he really carry out his threat?

Homework: Read to the end.

Unit III
Victor and Victim

1. The ending
Is the ending more or less what you expected it to be? Or did it come as a surprise?
What was your emotional reaction to it?
Since Montresor has done exactly what he has been threatening from the start, those who were surprised will have to acknowledge a certain resistance to the ultimate horror and/or a predisposition to look for a conventional happy ending or at least some sign that good will eventually triumph over evil. Which brings us to the next point.

2. Second reading/hearing of the whole story (recording: 18 minutes)
Before giving the students the opportunity of hearing (or reading) the story again, they should be asked to consider at least the first two of the questions listed under the next point.

3. Final discussion: the meaning
Has evil really triumphed?
Has Montresor really had his revenge?
Why does he "hesitate" before finishing his task? Why does his "heart grow sick"? (**9** 38, **10** 27–28)
Consider the two conditions for satisfactory revenge which Montresor mentions at the beginning of the story – have they been fulfilled?
What similarities can you find between Montresor and Fortunato?
What weakness has made Fortunato such an easy victim? Does Montresor share this weakness?
What is the significance of the Montresor family arms – seen in the light of the ending?
Consider the narrative situation: To whom (**5** 2–3) *is Montresor telling all this? When? How significant is this?*
Ideally, a number of these points will be brought up spontaneously by the students, and this will determine the sequence in which they are dealt with. In view of the inherent ambiguity of the ending, teachers should take care not to impose any one reading of it on the class, but allow for a variety of responses.

Daphne du Maurier

The Lordly Ones

1.

Ben was thought to be backward. He could not speak. When he tried to form words sounds came, harsh and ugly, and he did not know what to do with his tongue. He pointed when he wanted something, or fetched it for himself. They said he was tongue-tied, and that in a few years' time he would be taken to hospital and something could be done. His mother said he was sharp enough, he took in what you told him all right, and knew good from bad, but he was stubborn, he did not take kindly to "no". Because of his silence they forgot to explain things to him, arrivals and departures and changes of plan, and his world was made up of whims, the whims of older people. He would be told to dress for no reason, or to go out into the street to play; or some toy was denied him that had been given him an hour before.

When the stress became too great to bear he opened his mouth, and the sound that came out of it alarmed him even more than it alarmed his parents. Why did it rise? How did it come? Then someone, usually his mother, picked him up and shut him away in the cupboard under the stairs, amongst the mackintoshes and the shopping baskets, and he could hear her calling through the keyhole, "You'll stop there until you're quiet!" The noise would not be quelled. It did not belong to him. The anger was a force that had to have its way.

Later, crouched beside the keyhole, spent and tired, he would hear the noise die away, and peace would come to the cupboard. The fear would then be that his mother would go away and forget to let him out, and he would rattle the handle of the door to remind her. A flash of her skirt through the keyhole meant reassurance, and he would sit down and wait until the grinding of the key in the lock spelt release. Then he would step out into the daylight, blinking, and glance up at his mother to gauge her mood. If she was dusting or sweeping, she ignored him. All would be well until the next moment of anger or frustration, when the performance would be repeated – either the cupboard again, or his bedroom with no tea, his toys taken from him. The way to ensure against their anger was to please his parents, but this could not always be done, for the strain was too great. In the middle of play, absorbed, he forgot their commands.

One day suitcases were packed and he was dressed in his warmest clothes, although it was early spring, and they left the house in Exeter where he had been born and went to the moors. There had been talk about the moors for some weeks past.

"It's different up there from what it is down here," his parents would say. Somehow cajolery and threats were combined: one day he was to be lucky, another he had better not get out of sight once they moved. The very words "the moors" sounded dark and ominous, a sort of threat.

The bustle of departure added to fear. The rooms of his home, suddenly bare, were unfamiliar, and his mother, impatient, scolded him ceaselessly. She too wore different clothes, and an ugly hat. It clung round her ears, changing the shape of her face. As they left home she seized his hand, dragging it, and bewildered he watched his parents as they sat, anxious themselves, among the boxes and the packing-cases. Could it be that they were uncertain too? That none of them knew where they were going?

The train bore them away, but he could not see out of the windows. He was in the middle seat between his parents, and only the tops of trees told him of country. His mother gave him an orange he did not want. Forgetting caution, he threw it on the floor. She smacked him hard. The smack coincided with a sudden jolt of the train and the darkness of a tunnel, the two combined suggesting the cupboard under the stairs and punishment. He opened his mouth and the cry came from it.

As always, the sound brought panic. His mother shook him and he bit his tongue. The carriage was full of strangers. An old man behind a newspaper frowned. A woman, showing her teeth, offered him a green sweet. No one could be trusted. His cries became louder still and his mother, her face red, picked him up and took him into the rattling corridor. "Will you be quiet?" she shouted. All was confusion. Fatigue seized him, and he crumpled. Rage and fear made him stamp his feet, clad in new brown-laced shoes, adding to the clatter. The sound, coming from his belly, ceased; only the gasp for breath, the stifling sobs, told him that the pain was with him, but for what reason he could not tell.

"He's tired," somebody said.

They were back again in the carriage, and room was made for him by the window. The world outside went past. Houses clustered. He saw a road with cars upon it, and fields, then high banks swaying up and down. With the gradual slowing of the train his parents stood up and began to reach for their belongings. The fluster of departure was with them once again. The train ground to a standstill. Doors opened and clanged, and a porter shouted. They tumbled out on to the platform.

His mother clutched him by the hand and he peered up at her face, and at his father's too, to try and discover from their expressions whether what was happening was customary, expected by them, and if they knew what was to happen now. They climbed into a car, the luggage piled about them, and through the gathering dusk he understood that they were not back again in the town from which they had come, but in open country. The air bit sharp, cool-smelling, and his father turned with a laugh to him and said, "Can you smell the moors?"

The moors.... He tried to see from the window of the car, but a suitcase balked his view. His mother and father were talking amongst themselves. "She'll surely have put on a kettle for us, and give us a hand," said his mother; and, "We'll not unpack everything tonight. It will take days to get straight."

"I don't know," said his father. "It's surprising how different it will seem in a small house."

The road twisted, the car swaying at the corners. Ben felt sick. This would be the final disgrace. The sourness was coming and he shut his mouth. But the urge was too strong, and it came from him in a burst, splaying out over the car.

"Oh, no, that's too much," cried his mother, and she pushed him from her knee against the sharp end of the suitcase, bruising his cheek. His father tapped the window. "Stop ... the boy's been sick." The shame, the inevitable confusion of sickness, and with it the sudden cold so that he shivered. Everywhere lay the evidence of his shame, and an old cloth, evil-smelling, was produced by the driver to wipe his mouth.

On again, but slower now, standing between his father's knees, and at last the rutty, bumpy road came to an end and a light was in front of them.

"It's not raining, that's one blessing," said his mother. "Don't ask me what we'll do here when it does."

The small house stood alone, light in the windows. Ben, blinking and shivering still, climbed down from the car. He stood looking about him as the luggage was lifted out. For the moment he was ignored. The small house faced a green, smooth as a carpet in the dark, and behind the house, which was thatched, were humped black hills. The sharp sweet smell he had noticed on leaving the station was stronger still. He lifted his face to sniff the air. Where were the moors? He saw them as a band of brothers, powerful and friendly.

"Come on in, my handsome," said a woman from the house, and he did not draw back when she bore down upon him, welcoming and large, and led him into the paved kitchen. A stool was drawn up to the table and a glass of milk put in front of him. He sipped it slowly, his eyes sizing up the flagged kitchen, the scullery pump, the small latticed windows.

"Is he shy?" asked the woman, and the whispers began, the grown-up talk, something about his tongue. His father and his mother looked embarrassed and awkward. The woman glanced back again, in pity, and Ben dipped his face in his glass of milk. Then they forgot him, the dull talk passed him by, and unwatched he was able to eat bread and butter without hindrance, help himself to biscuits, his sickness gone and appetite returned.

"Oh yes, watch out for them," the woman said. "They're terrible thieves. They'll come by night and raid your larder, if you leave it open. Especially if it continues cold like this. Watch out for snow."

So the moors were robbers. A band of robbers wandering by night. Ben remembered the comic paper that his father had bought him, with the ogre's face upon the cover. Yet they could not be like that, for the woman was saying something about their fine looks.

"They won't hurt you," she said, "they're friendly enough." This to Ben, who watched her, puzzled. Then she laughed, and everyone got up to clear the tea, to unpack, to settle.

"Now then, don't wander off," said his mother. "If you don't behave you'll go straight to bed."

"He can't come to harm," the woman said. "I've latched the gate."

When they were not looking Ben slipped out of the open door and stood outside. The car that had brought them had disappeared. The silence, so different from the noise of the street at home, was like the silence that came when his parents were not angry. It wrapped itself about him. The little lights winking from the other cottages, away down the green, were distant as stars. He went and rested his chin on the gate, and stared into the peaceful darkness. He felt himself at rest. He had no wish to go indoors, to unpack his toys.

There must be a farm somewhere close, for the smell of manure mixed with the cold air, and a cow lowed from a stall. These discoveries were pleasing to him. Mostly he thought about the moors, the thieves of the night, but somehow they did not frighten him: the reassurance of the woman's smile and the way his parents had laughed showed that the moors were not to be feared. Anyway, it was to come to the moors that they had packed their things and left home. It was this that had been discussed now for so many weeks. "The boy will like the moors," people had said back at home. "He'll grow strong, up there. There's nothing like the moors for giving appetite."

It was true. Ben had eaten five pieces of bread and butter and three biscuits. Already the band of brothers had shown power. He wondered how close they were to the house, if they lurked, smiling encouragement, beyond those dark humped hills.

A sudden thought occurred to him. If food was put out for the thieves, they would not steal. They would eat it and be thankful. He went back inside the kitchen, and voices from upstairs told him that his parents and their helper were unpacking and out of the way. The table had been cleared, but the tea-things, unwashed, were piled in the scullery. There was a loaf of bread, a cake still uncut, and the remaining biscuits. Ben filled his pockets with the biscuits, and carried the loaf of bread and the cake. He went to the door, and so down the path to the gate. He set the food on the ground, and concentrated upon the task of unfastening the gate. It was easier than he had expected. He lifted the latch and the gate swung back. Then he picked up the loaf and the cake and went out on to the green. The thieves made for the green first, the woman had said. They prowled there, looking for odds and ends, and if nothing tempted them, and no one shouted and drove them away, they would come to the cottages.

Ben walked a few yards on to the green and set out the food. The thieves could not miss it if they came. They would be grateful, and go back to their lair in the black hills well satisfied. Looking back, he could see the figures of his parents moving backwards and forwards in the bedrooms upstairs. He jumped, to try the feel of the grass under his feet, more pleasing than a pavement, and lifted his face once more to feel the air. It came, cold and clean, from the hills. It was as though the moors knew, the thieves knew, that a feast was prepared for them. Ben was happy.

He ran back to the house, and as he did so his mother came downstairs.

"Come on, bed," she said.

Bed? So soon? His face protested, but she was not to be moved.

"There's enough to do without you round my heels," she complained.

She pulled him up the steep little stairway after her, and he saw his own bed, miraculously brought from home, standing in a corner of the small room lit by candlelight. It was close to the window, and his first thought was that he would be able to look out from his bed and watch when the thieves came. This interest kept him quiet while his mother helped him to undress, but she was rougher than usual. Her nails got caught in a button and scratched his skin, and when he whimpered she said sharply, "Oh, be quiet, do." The candle, stuck in a saucer, threw a monster shadow on the ceiling. It flounced his mother's figure to a grotesque shape.

"I'm too tired to wash you tonight," she said. "You'll have to stay dirty."

His father's voice called up the stairs. "What did you do with the bread and the cake?" he called. "I can't find them."

"They're on the scullery table," she answered. "I'll be down in a minute."

Ben realized that his parents would search for the food to put it away. Instinct warned him to make no sound. She finished undressing him, and he went straight to his bed without delay.

"Now I don't want to hear any more from you tonight," she said. "If you make a sound I'll send your father to you."

She went downstairs, taking the candle with her.

Ben was used to darkness, but, even so, the room was unfamiliar. He had not yet had time to learn the shape. Was there a chair? A table? Was it long or square? He lay back in bed biting at the blanket. He heard footsteps underneath his window. Sitting up, he looked between the curtains, and saw the woman who had welcomed them walk down the path, through the gate, and away down the road. She was carrying a lantern. She did not cross the green. The lantern danced as she moved, and soon she was swallowed up in the darkness. Only the bobbing light betrayed her passage.

Ben lay back again in bed, disturbed by the flickering lantern and voices raised in argument below. He heard his mother come upstairs. She threw open the door and stood there, holding the candle, the monstrous shadow behind her.

"Did you touch the tea things?" she said.

Ben made the sound his parents understood as a denial, but his mother was not satisfied. She came to the bed and, shielding her eyes, stared down at him.

"The bread and cake have gone," she said. "The biscuits too. You took them, didn't you? Where did you hide them?"

As always, the rising voice brought out antagonism. Ben shrank against his pillow and shut his eyes. It was not the way to question him. If she had smiled and made a joke of it, it would have been different.

"Very well," she said. "I'll settle you, young man."

She called for his father. Despair seized Ben. It would mean a whipping. He began to cry. Explanation was beyond him. He heard his father stump up the stairs and come into the room, his shadow monstrous too. The pair of them filled the small, unfamiliar room.

"Do you want a hiding?" his father asked. "Now then, what did you do with the bread?"

His father's face was ugly, worn with fatigue. The packing and unpacking, all the hustle of removal, of starting the new life, had meant strain. Ben sensed this, but he could not give way. He opened his mouth and yelled. The cry roused the full fatigue and anger of the father. Resentment, too. Why must his son be dumb?

"That's enough of that," he said.

He jerked Ben out of bed and stripped the pyjama legs. Then he laid the wriggling child across his knee. The hand found the flesh and hit hard, with all its force. Ben screamed louder still. The relentless hand, so large and powerful, smote and smote again.

"That's learned him, that's enough," said his mother. "There's neighbours across the green. We don't want trouble."

"He must know who's master," said his father, and it was not until his own hand ached with the force of the blows that he gave up and pushed Ben from his knee.

"Now holler if you dare," he said, rising abruptly, and Ben, face downwards on the bed, his sobs long ceased, heard them withdraw, felt the candle go, knew that the room was empty. Everything was pain. He tried to move his legs, but the movement sent a warning message to his brain. The pain travelled from his buttocks up his spine to the top of his head. No sound came from his lips now, only a trickle of tears from his eyes. Perhaps if he lay quite still the pain would go. He could not cover himself with the blanket, and the cold air found him, bringing its own dull ache.

Little by little the pain numbed. The tears dried on his cheeks. He had no thoughts at all, lying there on his face. He had forgotten the cause of his beating. He had forgotten the band of brothers, the thieves, the moors. If in a little while there could be nothing, let nothing come.

2.

He awoke suddenly, every sense alert. The moon shone through the gap in the curtains. At first he thought that everything was still, and the movement from the green outside told him they were there. They had come. He knew. Slowly, painfully, he dragged himself across his bed and so to the window. He pulled at the curtains. The white night showed him the wonder. The thieves were there, the lordly ones. Not as the woman had described them, but more beautiful. A little group, intent upon his offering. There was the mother, with two children, and another mother just behind, with a taller child, playing by himself. Two others ran round in circles, delighting in the snow, for with them the snow had come, turning the green white. That must be the father, watching. But he was not angry, like Ben's father: he was beautiful like the mothers and the children, beautiful and wise. He was staring at the window. He had already seen Ben, and then, to show his appreciation of the cake placed ready for him, he touched it gently and moved away, letting the son play with it instead.

It was the time of night when no one moves. Ben knew nothing of time, but instinct told him that his parents had long been in bed, and that morning would not come for many hours. He watched them, the moors, the lordly ones. They were not thieves at all, they were far too proud. They ate with delicacy what Ben had given them, and they did not attempt to come near to the house, or prowl, as the woman had said. Like Ben, they did not speak. They talked by signal. The father, in command, moved his head, and leaving the food the mothers summoned their children, and the whole company settled themselves on the green, in the snow, to wait for morning. Their supreme disdain of the sleeping houses showed itself to Ben as contempt of authority. They made their own laws.

Ben lowered himself from his bed. His buttocks and back were still very sore, and the cold night had stiffened him, lying as he had done without a cover. Nevertheless, he began to put on his clothes. He dressed slowly, not yet accustomed to doing it quite alone, but finally he satisfied himself that he was ready, although his jersey was back to front. Luckily his wellington boots were in the scullery. They had been among the first things to be unpacked.

He could see his room clearly now, for the moonlight turned it to day. There were no strange bulges or shapes. It was just a room, small and plain. The door-latch was high above his head, so he dragged a chair beneath it and stood on it to lift the latch.

Cunningly he crept down the narrow stair. Below in the kitchen it was still dark, but instinct led him to the scullery, and to the corner where his boots waited. He put them on. The larder was only a cupboard, part of the scullery, and the door was ajar. His mother, in her anger, must have forgotten to close it. Deliberately he took the last loaf, intended for breakfast, and then repeated his performance with the chair beneath the latch of the front door. There were bolts here too to be withdrawn. If his parents heard him, he was lost. He climbed down from the chair. The door lay open. The white night was before him, the great moon benign, and the lordly ones were waiting on the green. It was green no longer, but glistening white.

Softly, his boots lightly crunching the snow, Ben tiptoed down the path and lifted the latch of the gate. The sound roused the watchers on the green. One of the mothers looked up, and although she said nothing her movement warned the father, and he too turned his head. They waited to see what Ben would do. Perhaps, thought Ben, they hoped for further gifts: they had not brought food with them, and were hungry still.

He walked slowly towards them, holding out the loaf. The mother rose to her feet, and the children too. The action roused the others, and in a moment the little company, who had settled themselves for sleep, seemed ready to march once more. They did not try to take the bread from Ben. Some sense of delicacy, perhaps, forbade it. He wanted to show generosity to them and to flaunt his parents at the same time, so, tearing the loaf in two, he went to the smallest child, not much taller than himself, and offered him part of it. This surely would be understood.

The little moor came forward and took the bread, watching Ben when he had eaten it, and then he shook his hair out of his eyes, for he was wild and unkempt, and glanced at his mother. She did not do anything, she did not speak to him, and Ben, encouraged, offered her the other half of the loaf. She took it from him. Their silence pleased Ben, for it was something he understood and shared with them.

The mother had gold hair, like her ragged son, but the older boy was dark. Relationships were confusing, because there was another mother – or could it be an aunt? – who was standing quite close to the father, and a little apart, not taking much notice of anyone, was surely the gran, so grey and thin, who looked as if she did not care for the snow, but would have been more at her ease before a good warm fire. Ben wondered at their roaming ways. What made them wander, rather than stay at home? They were not thieves, he was sure they were not thieves.

Then the father gave a signal. He turned, and slowly, majestically, led the way down the green. The others followed, the children dancing, glad to be on the move again, and the old gran, hobbling, brought up the rear. Ben watched them, then glanced back at the sleeping house. Decision came to him. He was not going to stay with the parents who did not love him. He was going to follow the moors, the lordly ones.

Ben ran across the crunching snow in the wake of his chosen companions. The old gran looked over her shoulder as she heard him coming, but she did not mind. She seemed to accept him. Ben ran until he caught up with the mother he liked best, the one with the golden hair and the ragged son, and when he was beside her she gave him a friendly nod of the head to show that he was now of the company. Ben trudged beside her in the snow. The father, still in front, was making for the hills, but he had a fine instinct for avoiding the deeper snow. He picked his way along a track, drifts on either side, and came at last to a high ridge where the world stretched wide and far on either side. The green was a long way below. Soon it was lost to sight. There were no houses in this wild country, lit by moonlight. Ben was warm from his climb, and so were his companions. Their breath went from them all like smoke in the frosted air.

What now? They looked to the father for instructions. He seemed to debate the move within himself. He glanced to right and to left. Then he decided to continue along the ridge, and once more led the way, with the family following.

The children dragged a little, for they were getting tired, and Ben, to encourage them, jumped and skipped, forgetting his bruises, stiff back. The pain made him cry out, and the cry startled the golden mother, who, staring at him, spoke to him. Was she asking a question? Ben did not understand her language. He thought that the noises in his throat must have told the mother that his back was stiff, for she seemed reassured and slowed her walk to his. Ben was relieved. He did not want to have to hobble in the rear with the old gran.

Presently the ridge sloped to an old trackway, banked high on either side with snow, and the father stopped here, making as though to camp. He stared across the wastes to the line of distant hills, and did not move. He must be thinking very deeply, decided Ben; he did not want to talk to the others. The mothers wandered around in circles, and then found a resting-place for the children on firm ground against a bank of frozen snow. The old gran, discontented, could not settle. She found the night air cold. Ben wondered what he should do. His legs were aching and he was as tired as the gran. He watched the children curl up in a patch of snow. If they can do that, he thought to himself, I suppose I can too. But they are used to sleeping on the ground, and I am not.

Then the mother, the one he liked, decided to settle by her son. Her broad, comfortable body reminded Ben of the woman who had welcomed him and his parents the night before at the thatched house on the green. She had been kindly too. But this mother was beautiful, more beautiful by far than his own mother. He hesitated a moment, then he crept forward and crouched against her. Would she be angry? Would she push him away?

She did not look at him. She did not speak. She let him understand that he could lie there, against her, and receive her warmth. Her good body smell was comforting. He snuggled close, his head against her shoulder, and put up his hand to touch her hair. She shook her head gently, and sighed. Ben closed his eyes, eased by the warmth, the comfort, the tender understanding of the mother and the reassurance of the father, still watching the far hills. He was the guardian of his sons, he would never beat them. They were all of one company, these moors, not the band of brothers he had imagined, but a family, a tribe, belonging one to the other. He would never leave them, the lordly ones.

3.

The sun came over the hills in splendour, and Ben opened his eyes. In a moment it was broad day. Already the old gran was on the move, hobbling about on her stiff legs. Her example put the others to shame, and they rose in turn, the children reluctantly, for they could have done with an hour or two more of sleep. No one had breakfast, and Ben was hungry. What was to be done about food? The bread he had brought with him had all been finished on the green. Uneasily, he remembered that the woman had called them thieves. Perhaps, after all, it was true. They were going to wait until night, and then descend to a village and either beg for bread or steal it. What about the children? Would they last through the day?

Ben stood up and stamped his feet for warmth. Then he stared. The little ragged son, who must surely be of an age with himself, was feeding from his mother. Only babies did that. Was it because the lordly ones were wanderers that they had such wild ways? The mother did not hide herself with her son to do this, as a friend of his own mother's had once done in their back kitchen, but she let it happen now, in the open, with the others looking on. Then abruptly she pushed the small son away, showing him that he had had enough. She began to walk after the father. The long trail started, and Ben stumped along by the mother's side. After all, if it was their custom...

He began to wish the mother had fed him too. The ragged son, filled and happy, danced up to him, suggesting play, and Ben, forgetting his hunger, ran after him, laughing, pulling at his hair. They ran in circles, calling to one another. And the ragged son, as he might have done himself, pranced back to tease the gran. He skipped in front of her, mocking the hobbling gait, and nobody minded, thought Ben, nobody told him it was rude.

The sun was high now, the warmth of it melting the snow beneath, and with it came the gnawing pain of hunger in Ben's stomach, and there was nothing to eat, for the lordly ones gave him nothing. Quelling his shyness, he went to the mother and pointed, showing by the sound in his throat that he wanted to feed. She moved away, though, she would not let him. He understood that she kept her food for the son.

They went on walking, they followed the father. He was some way ahead when he suddenly stopped, and, looking back, called to the mothers. They halted, and the mothers returned his cry. Then they waited. Instructions had been given not to move. There was a sound of running in the far distance, and over the hill came another moor, a stranger. He stopped when he saw the father, and the pair of them stared at each other. The mother beside Ben murmured something to her companion, and the company formed a little circle, wondering what the father was going to do.

Ben watched, apprehensive; he did not like the look of the threatening stranger. The newcomer advanced again, and then, without warning, hurled himself upon the father, and the pair of them wrestled there together in the snow, fiercely, without weapons, the watchful father turning of a sudden to a savage. There was a time of anger, and stamping feet and strangled sobs, and the mothers, watching, huddled together for comfort, Ben in the midst of them. Their fear bred fear in Ben, and he began to cry again, remembering his own angry father. Would the battle never be done? Suddenly it was over. But the result was terror. For the father, the kind leader who had watched over them all night, began to run. Not towards his own family, the mothers and the children, but away across the snow to the distant hills. He was afraid of the stranger. The stranger had defeated him. As Ben watched he saw the trail of blood on the snow.

Ben put out his hand and touched the mother. He tried to tell her that they must follow the wounded father, follow their leader, but she shook herself away impatiently. She was looking at the conqueror. Slowly he advanced towards them. Ben shrank back against the ragged son, as frightened, surely, as he. The old gran turned away in disgust. She would have nothing to do with it. Then the mother, the golden mother beside whom Ben had slept, walked slowly towards the stranger, and Ben realized, by the way she touched him, that she acknowledged him as leader. He would be the father from now on. What if it happened in his own home? What if a neighbour came to fight with his father, and, beating him, drove him away from home? Would his mother mind, would she go to the neighbour?

Ben waited and watched, and then the stranger, who was brown-haired and broad, less graceful than the defeated father, but younger, jerked his head in signal to the mothers to follow him, and meekly, without a word, they obeyed, the children with them. Only the old gran looked backwards across the snow, where, in the distance, stood the smudged figure of the defeated leader, lost and alone.

The battle was over. The day went on as before. As Ben trudged beside his companions through the snow he became accustomed to the new father, the new leader. By afternoon he might have led them always. Perhaps after all he was a relation, an uncle – there was no way of telling what customs they had, the moors.

The sun travelled across the sky and began to sink on the other side of the hills. The company paused once more, and the new father, not so watchful as the first, walked round about the other mother, the aunt – he seemed to like her best. He did not stay on guard as the first father had done. They murmured together, sharing some secret, and when one of the children ran to join them the new father drove him away. He was not going to be so easy of temper as the first.

Ben was faint from hunger now. He went to the mother, the one he knew, the mother of the ragged son, and this time she was patient while he tried to feed, and did not push him away, but suffered him to stay. Ben managed to feed a little, but it was hard. He was not certain of himself, and he was clumsy. After a moment or two the mother moved, and then, as she had done the night before, she settled herself in the snow with her son, and Ben lay down beside her. The others waited around, but Ben had already closed his eyes, his head once more against the shoulder of the mother, his hand in her hair, and whether or not they settled he did not know. Nor did he bother about it, for all that mattered was to be warm and sheltered, protected and cherished by the one he loved.

The angry shouts brought the company to their feet. Bewildered, Ben rubbed his eyes. The moon was full. There, running across the snow, was a crowd of men with sticks, his own father among them, and they were shouting and yelling, waving their sticks at the lordly ones.

This time there was no battle. The leader ran. And with him galloped the mothers, the children, the old gran. They galloped quickly under the moonlight across the frozen snow, and Ben, deserted by his mother, the chestnut mare, deserted by his brothers the moors, the lordly ones, uttered a great cry. He heard the cry tear his chest, and he shouted, "No ... no ... no ..." for the first and the last time, and he fell face downwards in the snow.

Biographical Notes

Daphne du Maurier was born in 1907, into a family with a strong literary tradition. Her father, Sir Gerald du Maurier, was a well-known actor and theatre manager; her half-French grandfather, George du Maurier, was a famous novelist. She was educated at home and in Paris.

At the age of 21 she began writing stories, and three years later her first novel, The Loving Spirit, *was published. Many more were of follow, including several best-sellers. Her genious for conveying an air of mystery and*

du Maurier, The Lordly Ones

wonder with a strong touch of the macabre has made her one of the most popular authors of the century. Her novel **Rebecca**, *published in 1938, has since been translated into over twenty languages, and filmed under the direction of Alfred Hitchcock. Another Hitchcock classic is based on her story "The Birds".*

"The Lordly Ones" is taken from a collection of stories published in 1959. As well as fiction, Daphne du Maurier has also written plays, articles and biographies.

In 1959 she was made a Dame of the British Empire (D.B.E.). Now widowed, she has three children and seven grandchildren.

Annotations

15	1	backward	mentally retarded
	9	whim	sudden wish, lacking logic and reason
	18	to quell	to suppress
	20	**to crouch** [aʊ]	to bend down
	24	**reassurance**	making sure again (that everything was all right)
	25	spelt release	meant that he would be freed
	26	to gauge [geɪdʒ]	to measure roughly, to estimate
	31	**strain**	mental stress
16	3	moor	1. land covered with turf and heather
			2. dark-skinned person from north Africa
	6	cajolery	gentle persuasion
	9	bustle ['bʌsl]	(often "hustle and bustle") a lot of unnecessary activity
	10	**to scold** [əʊ]	to speak angrily (to a child)
	13	**bewildered** [ɪ]	puzzled, confused
	19	to smack	to hit with an open hand
		to coincide with	to happen at the same time as
	20	jolt [əʊ]	sudden movement
	28	fatigue [fə'tiːg]	tiredness
		to crumple	*here*: to collapse
	29	clad	dressed
	31	to stifle [aɪ]	to stop one's breath
		sob	a short catch of breath (when crying)
	35	to cluster	to appear in groups
	38	fluster	confusion, a lot of activity
17	3	**customary**	usual
	5	**dusk**	partial darkness after sunset
	10	to balk [bɔːk]	to hinder
	17	**disgrace**	shame
	18	to splay	to spread out
	21	**to bruise** [uː]	to hurt the skin, leaving a mark on it
	22	**inevitable** [-'----]	unavoidable

	27	rutty	with ruts (worn-down tracks) in it
	34	thatched	with a roof made of straw or reeds
	39	to bear down on	(of a large person or object) to approach
	40	paved, flagged	with a floor of flat stones
18	2	scullery	small kitchen where things are washed and stored
		latticed	covered with crossed wooden strips
	10	**to raid**	to break in and steal things
		larder	place where food is stored
	13	ogre [ˈəʊgə]	monster
	21	to latch	to close the latch (a bar for locking s.th.)
	30	manure [məˈnjʊə]	dung
	31	to low	to moo
19	1	to lurk	to wait in hiding
	14	to prowl [aʊ]	to move about secretly, in search of s.th.
	19	lair	den, hiding place
	37	to flounce	*here*: to enlarge, to spread out (like a flounced skirt)
20	15	to bob	to move up and down
	26	antagonism	hostile feelings
	31	to stump	to walk heavily
	34	**a hiding**	a beating
	39	**to rouse** [aʊ]	to awaken, to give rise to
		resentment	a feeling that s.th. is unfair
	40	dumb [dʌm]	unable to speak
21	2	**to jerk**	to make a sharp movement
	3	to wriggle	to move about trying to free o.s.
	4	relentless	merciless, not stopping
	5	to smite, smote, smitten	to hit
	11	to holler	to shout, to yell
	15	buttocks	bottom, backside
		spine	backbone
	19	to numb [nʌm]	(of a feeling) to disappear, to go away
	29	intent upon	concentrating on
	36	**appreciation**	liking, thankfulness for
22	5	delicacy	fine manners or movements
	10	**disdain**	contempt for, lack of interest in
	16	jersey	sweater, pullover
		wellington boots	rubber boots
	20	**bulge**	s.th. swelling outwards from a surface
	23	**cunning**	sly, clever
	26	ajar [–ˈ–]	open
	31	benign [bɪˈnaɪn]	friendly
	33	**to tiptoe**	to walk on the tips of one's toes
23	4	to flaunt	(*non-standard usage*) to flout, to disobey
	9	unkempt	untidy (of hair, clothes)
	16	gran	grandmother
	18	**to roam**	to wander
	23	to hobble	to walk with difficulty
		to bring up the rear	to be the last

	27	in the wake of	after, following the tracks of
	32	to trudge	to move heavily, as if tired
	34	drift	snow blown by the wind into a pile
	35	**ridge**	raised land, sloping down on two sides
24	20	to curl up	to make o.s. small
	31	to snuggle	to move close to a person's body
25	1	splendour	glory
	4	**reluctantly**	unwillingly
	24	to prance	to move as if dancing
	25	**to tease**	to make fun of, to play tricks on
		gait	way of walking
	28	gnawing ['nɔːɪŋ]	*here*: tormenting
26	3	apprehensive	worrying about what is going to happen
	4	to hurl	to throw
	5	**to wrestle**	to fight, trying to force the other person to the ground
	7	**savage** ['sævɪdʒ]	wild person
	8	to huddle	to move close together
	9	to breed, bred	to make grow
	23	**to acknowledge**	to accept, to recognize
	29	**meek**	humble and obedient
	31	smudged	*here*: not clear, not easy to recognize
27	5	**faint**	weak
	9	**clumsy**	awkward in one's movements
	15	to cherish	to love, to care for
	22	chestnut ['tʃesnʌt]	reddish-brown, the colour of chestnuts
	23	mare	female horse

Interpretation and Teaching Notes

Background, Content and Analysis

"Ben was thought to be backward" (**15** 1). This very first sentence tells of a misunderstanding, and in doing so, sets the scene for a story which practically consists of misunderstandings. An alert reader will be able to identify and disentangle many of them, but only at the end of the story will it emerge to what extent even the reader has been caught up in the tangled web.

The events of the story cover two days, beginning with a family's departure for a spring holiday in the moors and ending with their son being rescued from a herd of wild horses. The area in question could be any of the uplands of south-west England, e.g. Dartmoor or Exmoor. This familiar countryside provides the highly atmospheric setting of many of the author's stories and novels. Herds of wild horses are still one of the more striking features of these Devonshire moors.

That the ending should come as a surprise results from a story-telling technique which Daphne du Maurier has used to similar effect in at least one other story, "The Old Man"[1]. It involves a deliberate manipulation of the reader's perception of events.

The person at the centre of the confusion is a boy of indeterminate age – one reader's guess being around five or six – and apparently an only son. But equally important for the course of events are his parents, and their failure to come to terms with the boy's handicap, to understand his needs and communicate with him adequately.

That backwardness in the sense of mental retardation is not Ben's real problem is made adequately clear in the course of the first two paragraphs. He is dumb (**15** 1–3), i.e. unable to speak. And he is apparently emotionally disturbed (**15** 12–14, 17–19). The reasons for his tantrums seem quite plausible: assuming that he is not capable of understanding, nobody explains anything to him, so that he is constantly at the mercy of "the whims of older people" (**15** 9). And the crude punishments which his tantrums bring on him (**15** 14–17, 28–30) only serve to make the world a more terrifying and incomprehensible place.

After the initial introduction (i.e. from about the second paragraph on) the author restricts our perspective to Ben's point of view, so that we share his perception of this terrifying world. This encourages sympathy, and

---

[1] "The Old Man" is included in *The Birds and Other Stories* (Penguin Books). A simplified version of this story is included in the Listening Comprehension collection (book and cassette) *What's That Again?* Stuttgart: Klett, 1980.

understanding for his efforts to make sense of the apparent confusion. Even the most fantastic of his wild guesses retain a certain plausibility, given the scrappiness of the information available to him. Whatever Ben lacks, it is not intelligence or imagination.

With the help of our superior knowledge we are, of course, able to mentally correct his misunderstandings, or at least to recognize them as such. We are familiar with the nervous excitement that often surrounds the preparations for a holiday, and we know what going to the moors means. But without this knowledge and experience it could certainly seem that everybody is nervously preparing for a journey into the unknown (**16** 14–15) and that there is something ominous about the "moors" (**16** 7–8).

Our awareness of the second meaning of the word "moors" prepares us for what follows. It emerges that the boy is interpreting the snippets of conversation he hears as referring to some kind of fellow-creatures (**17** 36–37). That he should be gradually building up a favourable picture of them as a "band of brothers, powerful and friendly" is due to coincidence. After a journey fraught with frustation and confusion (he throws a tantrum in the train and is sick in the car), the house they arrive at is pleasant and peaceful, the typical smell of the countryside is pleasant, and the woman who greets them is friendly (**17** 32–**18** 8).

Subsequent adult chit-chat apparently referring to thieving though otherwise harmless gypsies is overheard by Ben and linked in his mind with this already imagined "band of brothers", whose influence is supposed to be so benificial. "There's nothing like the moors for giving appetite," people had said, and this now seems to be true (**18** 36–**19** 2).

The next logical step for Ben is to court their favour. He decides to get food from the kitchen and put it out on the green, where the woman had said the thieves would be. This, of course, leads to disaster. His parents are furious when they discover that food is missing, he can't explain, and part one of the story ends with a cruel beating, tears and sleep.

Part two covers the events of that night, and includes the turning point where even otherwise alert readers are likely to be led astray by the boy's distorted perception of these events – and by the author's selective presentation of them. Ben wakes in the middle of the night to see his "moors" arrive on the green, and is gratified to see that they are even more beautiful than he had imagined (**21** 27–34). They are "the lordly ones" (**21** 28), proud, silent, and with a "supreme disdain of the sleeping houses" (**22** 10).

More important, the father is "not angry, like Ben's father" (**21** 33). Still sore from last night's beating, Ben is strongly drawn to these superior creatures. He dresses with some difficulty, and quietly makes his way out of the house, carrying a further offering. Snow has fallen on the green, though it is early spring.

Somewhat shy at first, the "moors" finally accept the bread Ben offers them and seem to accept him as one of themselves. Their silence seems particularly attractive to the dumb boy (**23** 11–12). Inevitably, when the group begins to move away, Ben decides to go with them. This section of the story ends on a comforting note, with Ben snuggled up against the mother "moor" to sleep, and vowing never to leave the lordly ones.

The third and final part of the story deals with the less satisfactory events of the following day. Hunger is the first problem which results from the group's irregular habits. Ben's desperate attempt to breast-feed with the other children is rejected (**25** 29–32). Worse still, a fight ensues which results in the father's place being taken by a less congenial stranger.

By nightfall everything seems all right again – Ben has even been allowed to breast-feed. But then the group is disturbed by a group of men, including Ben's father, "waving their sticks at the lordly ones" (**27** 19).

And it is only at this point that Daphne du Maurier abandons the carefully selective vocabulary she has been using up to now and lets us see the "moors" through the adults' eyes instead of Ben's. The gold-haired mother and her ragged son (e.g. **23** 13) could well have been the gypsies that most readers will have assumed them to be. But now the mother is the "chestnut mare" (**27** 22) and they not only run, but "gallop" (**27** 20–21) across the frozen snow.

Ben, of course, is not aware of any change in their status. For him the rescue means betrayal. Deserted by the lordly ones, he utters the first intelligible word of his life: "No ..." (**27** 24–25). It is also his last – and we are left to imagine what that means. Either he dies of shock, or he lives, but never speaks again.

It hardly matters how one reads the last line. The latter interpretation may be less tragic in the normal sense, but it has more of the inevitability of classic tragedy. And for a boy who had just begun to establish some kind of emotional contact with his surroundings, a lapse into total silence is indeed a kind of death.

Recommended Teaching Units (Overview)

I. Home preparation to **17** 29 (exposition: Ben, his handicap and his parents; journey to the moors – word not understood); discussion of narrative technique and point of view.

II. Home preparation up to end of part 1, discussion of content (arrival at house on the moors, Ben imagines moors as mysterious beings, decision to appease them, steals food, punishment); speculation about further developments.

III. Home preparation up to end of part 2, discussion of content (Ben runs away with the "moors" – happy).

IV. Home preparation to end of story (problems in adapting to the "moors'" strange ways, the fight, hunger, the rescue); discussion of effect of ending and how achieved.

Unit I
Ben

Preparation: The students should have read to **17** 29.

1. Narrative technique and point of view
Who is the narrator of the story?
From what point of view is it told?
It should be clear from the facts mentioned in the first paragraph that the story is told by an "omniscient" author-narrator who could, if she wished, give us full access to all the characters thoughts, but who chooses to restrict the point of view (at least from the second paragraph on) to that of Ben.

2. Ben
Who is Ben?
What is his parents' attitude to him?
How does he behave when punished or frustrated?
These are pure comprehension questions. The following call for some degree of interpretation – or even speculation – mainly on the basis of the information given in the first page.
What exactly is his handicap?
How intelligent is he? How imaginative?
What do you think his (mental) age is?

3. The journey (comprehension)
Where is the journey to?
At what time of year is it undertaken?
What means of transport is used?
What goes wrong on the way?

4. Ben's feelings
What is the main reason for Ben's tantrum on the train?
Can you understand his reaction?
Describe his feelings about going on the journey.
The main point to be stressed here is the lack of information which makes the world a terrifyng place for Ben. It may be advisable to re-read in class

45

the passages that express the boy's confusion and ambivalent feelings about going to the moors (**16** 5–14, **17** 6–10).

Homework: Read to the end of part 1 (**21** 22).

Unit II
Misunderstandings

1. Arrival (comprehension)
Describe the house the family arrive at (as seen by Ben).
Who welcomes them?
What impression does she make on Ben?
What makes Ben feel better?

2. Misunderstandings
What do the adults talk about while Ben is eating?
*Who do you think the "thieves" (***18** 9) *are?*
Who does Ben understand them to be talking about?
What does Ben find especially puzzling about their talk?
How reasonable is Ben's interpretation?
Why does Ben come to the conclusion that the "moors" are not to be feared?
It should be noted that the train of thought by which Ben draws his conclusions is quite logical. Attention should be drawn to the double meaning of the word "moors", which can refer to an exotic race of dark-skinned people, not unlike the gypsies that were presumably referred to in the overheard conversation.

3. Ben's plan (comprehension)
What idea occurs to Ben to prevent the "moors" from stealing?
How does he go about it?
How does he feel about having done it?
What do his parents discover?
How do they react?
How does Ben react to their accusations?
What makes the father so angry?
How does he punish Ben?
What are Ben's feelings as he lies in bed?

4. Speculation
What do you think this incident will lead to?
It is not unlikely that some students will hit on the idea that Ben will run away from home, possibly with the gypsies/moors that he imagines to be a

"band of brothers". The teacher should not, however, try to influence their speculation in any way.

Homework: Read part 2 (to **24** 38).

Unit III
The Moors

Note: While dealing with this section, the teacher should make the effort to play Daphne du Maurier's game and use only words that can refer equally to people and animals. If, however, the students happen to introduce specifically human vocabulary (e.g. people, person, man, woman, boy, girl, gypsy), they should not be corrected.

1. Comprehension questions
What wakes Ben during the night?
What does he think has happened?
What does he see when he looks out of the window?
What new name does he give his imagined friends?
How many of them are there? What ages, sexes, etc.?
Do they live up to his expectations?
How do the "moors" react to the gift he has left out for them?
What impression does their behaviour make on him?
What does Ben do then? Describe how he goes about it.
How do the "moors" react to his presence?
What does he find easy/hard to understand about their habits?
When they move to go away, what decision does Ben come to?
What reasons are given for his decision?
Where does the father lead them?
What makes the trek difficult for Ben?
How does he feel when they settle down to sleep?

2. Sympathy and suspense
*Describe your reaction to the passage where Ben creeps out of the house (**22** 12–34). What did you want to happen? What did you fear would happen? Why?*
It should emerge that in Ben, the author has created a credible character that readers have to sympathize with; sharing his point of view leads to almost total identification with his hopes and fears – which makes for considerable suspense. The following discussion points should underline this aspect.
Can you understand Ben's decision?
Do you think he is right to go with his new friends? Or do you fear it is a mistake?

Are there any passages you found particularly moving?

Homework: Read part 3 (to end).
Alternative: Particularly if a double period is available, it may be preferred to read and discuss the ending in class. This will call for the points of Unit IV to be dealt with in an altered sequence and in a more cursory fashion, and more emphasis to be put on the gradual turn for the worse in the course of the following day.

Unit IV
The Ending

1. Comprehension and immediate reactions
What do you now know about the moors?
When did you realize the truth? Could/should you have realized it earlier?
What hints were given in this last section of the story as to the true nature of the "moors"?
In retrospect it should seem obvious that the way of life actually described is not quite what one would expect of gypsies: there has been a progression from moderately plausible (sleeping in the snow, part 2) to most unlikely (the incidents of part 3). If we have accepted the typical behaviour of a herd of horses (the fight, etc.) as possible human behaviour, we are strongly under the influence of the narrative point of view.

2. Significance of the ending (discussion)
What actually happens to Ben at the end?
The ending is truly ambiguous – but the less drastic reading of it may be found more satisfactory. A lapse into total silence is certainly tragic enough.

3. Narrative technique (discussion)
How did the author avoid revealing that the "moors" were really a herd of wild horses?
Pick out the words and phrases she has used to refer to the creatures.
Do you feel tricked by this? Or is this technique legitimate?

Shirley Jackson

The Lottery

The morning of June 27th was clear and sunny, with the fresh warmth of a full-summer day; the flowers were blossoming profusely and the grass was richly green. The people of the village began to gather in the square, between the post office and the bank, around ten o'clock; in some towns there were so many people that the lottery took two days and had to be started on June 26th, but in this village, where there were only about three hundred people, the whole lottery took less than two hours, so it could begin at ten o'clock in the morning and still be through in time to allow the villagers to get home for noon dinner.

The children assembled first, of course. School was recently over for the summer, and the feeling of liberty sat uneasily on most of them; they tended to gather together quietly for a while before they broke into boisterous play, and their talk was still of the classroom and the teacher, of books and reprimands. Bobby Martin had already stuffed his pockets full of stones, and the other boys soon followed his example, selecting the smoothest and roundest stones; Bobby and Harry Jones and Dickie Delacroix – the villagers pronounced this name "Dellacroy" – eventually made a great pile of stones in one corner of the square and guarded it against the raids of the other boys. The girls stood aside, talking among themselves, looking over their shoulders at the boys, and the very small children rolled in the dust or clung to the hands of their older brothers or sisters.

Soon the men began to gather, surveying their own children, speaking of planting and rain, tractors and taxes. They stood together, away from the pile of stones in the corner, and their jokes were quiet and they smiled rather than laughed. The women, wearing faded house dresses and sweaters, came shortly after their menfolk. They greeted one another and exchanged bits of gossip as they went to join their husbands. Soon the women, standing by their husbands, began to call to their children, and the children came reluctantly, having to be called four or five times. Bobby Martin ducked under his mother's grasping hand and ran, laughing, back to the pile of stones. His father spoke up sharply, and Bobby came quickly and took his place between his father and his oldest brother.

The lottery was conducted – as were the square dances, the teenage club, the Halloween program – by Mr. Summers, who had time and energy to devote to civic activities. He was a round-faced, jovial man and he ran the coal business, and people were sorry for him, because he had no children and his wife was a scold. When he arrived in the square, carrying the black wooden box, there was a murmur of conversation among the villagers, and he waved and called, "Little late today, folks". The postmaster, Mr. Graves, followed him, carrying a three-legged stool, and the stool was put in the center of the square and Mr. Summers set the black box down on it. The villagers kept their distance, leaving a space between themselves and the stool, and when Mr. Summers said, "Some of you fellows want to give me a hand?" there was a hesitation before two men, Mr. Martin and his oldest son, Baxter, came forward to hold the box steady on the stool while Mr. Summers stirred up the papers inside it.

The original paraphernalia for the lottery had been lost long ago, and the black box now resting on the stool had been put into use even before Old Man Warner, the oldest man in town, was born. Mr. Summers spoke frequently to the villagers about making a new box, but no one liked to upset even as much tradition as was represented by the black box. There was a story that the present box had been made with some pieces of the box that had preceded it, the one that had been constructed when the first people settled down to make a village here. Every year, after the lottery, Mr. Summers began talking again about a new box, but every year the subject was allowed to fade off without anything's being done. The black box grew shabbier each year; by now it was no longer completely black but splintered badly along one side to show the original wood color, and in some places faded or stained.

Mr. Martin and his oldest son, Baxter, held the black box securely on the stool until Mr. Summers had stirred the papers thoroughly with his hand. Because so much of the ritual had been forgotten or discarded, Mr. Summers had been successful in having slips of paper substituted for the chips of wood that had been used for generations. Chips of wood, Mr. Summers had argued, had been all very well when the village was tiny, but now that the population was more than three hundred and likely to keep on growing, it was necessary to use something that would fit more easily into the black box. The night before the lottery, Mr. Summers and Mr. Graves made up the slips of paper and put them in the box, and it was then taken to the safe of Mr. Summers's coal company and locked up until Mr. Summers was ready to take it to the square next morning. The rest of the year, the box was put away, sometimes one place, sometimes another; it had spent one year in Mr.

Graves's barn and another year underfoot in the post office, and sometimes it was set on a shelf in the Martin grocery and left there.

There was a great deal of fussing to be done before Mr. Summers declared the lottery open. There were the lists to make up – of heads of families, heads of households in each family, members of each household in each family. There was the proper swearing-in of Mr. Summers by the postmaster, as the official of the lottery; at one time, some people remembered, there had been a recital of some sort, performed by the official of the lottery, a perfunctory, tuneless chant that had been rattled off duly each year; some people believed that the official of the lottery used to stand just so when he said or sang it, others believed that he was supposed to walk among the people, but years and years ago this part of the ritual had been allowed to lapse. There had been, also, a ritual salute, which the official of the lottery had had to use in addressing each person who came up to draw from the box, but this also had changed with time, until now it was felt necessary only for the official to speak to each person approaching. Mr. Summers was very good at all this; in his clean white shirt and blue jeans, with one hand resting carelessly on the black box, he seemed very proper and important as he talked interminably to Mr. Graves and the Martins.

Just as Mr. Summers finally left off talking and turned to the assembled villagers, Mrs. Hutchinson came hurriedly along the path to the square, her sweater thrown over her shoulders, and slid into place in the back of the crowd. "Clean forgot what day it was," she said to Mrs. Delacroix, who stood next to her, and they both laughed softly. "Thought my old man was out back stacking wood." Mrs. Hutchinson went on, "and then I looked out the window and the kids was gone, and then I remembered it was the twenty-seventh and came a-running." She dried her hands on her apron, and Mrs. Delacroix said, "You're in time, though. They're still talking away up there."

Mrs. Hutchinson craned her neck to see through the crowd and found her husband and children standing near the front. She tapped Mrs. Delacroix on the arm as a farewell and began to make her way through the crowd. The people separated good-humoredly to let her through; two or three people said, in voices just loud enough to be heard across the crowd, "Here comes your Missus, Hutchinson," and "Bill, she made it after all." Mrs. Hutchinson reached her husband, and Mr. Summers, who had been waiting, said cheerfully, "Thought we were going to have to get on without you, Tessie." Mrs. Hutchinson said, grinning, "Wouldn't have me leave m'dishes in the sink, now, would you, Joe?" and soft laughter ran through the crowd as the people stirred back into position after Mrs. Hutchinson's arrival.

"Well, now," Mr. Summers said soberly, "guess we better get started, get this over with, so's we can go back to work. Anybody ain't here?"

"Dunbar," several people said. "Dunbar, Dunbar."

Mr. Summers consulted his list. "Clyde Dunbar," he said. "That's right. He's broke his leg, hasn't he? Who's drawing for him?"

"Me, I guess," a woman said, and Mr. Summers turned to look at her. "Wife draws for her husband," Mr. Summers said. "Don't you have a grown boy to do it for you, Janey?" Although Mr. Summers and everyone else in the village knew the answer perfectly well, it was the business of the official of the lottery to ask such questions formally. Mr. Summers waited with an expression of polite interest while Mrs. Dunbar answered.

"Horace's not but sixteen yet," Mrs. Dunbar said regretfully. "Guess I gotta fill in for the old man this year."

"Right," Mr. Summers said. He made a note on the list he was holding. Then he asked, "Watson boy drawing this year?"

A tall boy in the crowd raised his hand. "Here," he said. "I'm drawing for m'mother and me." He blinked his eyes nervously and ducked his head as several voices in the crowd said things like "Good fellow, Jack," and "Glad to see your mother's got a man to do it."

"Well," Mr. Summers said, "guess that's everyone. Old Man Warner make it?"

"Here," a voice said, and Mr. Summers nodded.

A sudden hush fell on the crowd as Mr. Summers cleared his throat and looked at the list. "All ready?" he called. "Now, I'll read the names – heads of families first – and the men come up and take a paper out of the box. Keep the paper folded in your hand without looking at it until everyone has had a turn. Everything clear?"

The people had done it so many times that they only half listened to the directions; most of them were quiet, wetting their lips, not looking around. Then Mr. Summers raised one hand high and said, "Adams." A man disengaged himself from the crowd and came forward. "Hi, Steve," Mr. Summers said, and Mr. Adams said, "Hi, Joe." They grinned at one another humorlessly and nervously. Then Mr. Adams reached into the black box and took out a folded paper. He held it firmly by one corner as he turned and went hastily back to his place in the crowd, where he stood a little apart from his family, not looking down at his hand.

"Allen," Mr. Summers said. "Anderson ... Bentham."

"Seems like there's no time at all between lotteries any more," Mrs. Delacroix said to Mrs. Graves in the back row. "Seems like we got through with the last one only last week."

"Time sure goes fast," Mrs. Graves said.

"Clark.... Delacroix."

"There goes my old man," Mrs. Delacroix said. She held her breath while her husband went forward.

"Dunbar," Mr. Summers said, and Mrs. Dunbar went steadily to the box while one of the women said, "Go on, Janey," and another said, "There she goes."

"We're next," Mrs. Graves said. She watched while Mr. Graves came around from the side of the box, greeted Mr. Summers gravely, and selected a slip of paper from the box. By now, all through the crowd there were men holding the small folded papers in their large hands, turning them over and over nervously. Mrs. Dunbar and her two sons stood together, Mrs. Dunbar holding the slip of paper.

"Harburt.... Hutchinson."

"Get up there, Bill," Mrs. Hutchinson said, and the people near her laughed.

"Jones."

"They do say," Mr. Adams said to Old Man Warner, who stood next to him, "that over in the north village they're talking of giving up the lottery."

Old Man Warner snorted. "Pack of crazy fools," he said. "Listening to the young folks, nothing's good enough for *them*. Next thing you know, they'll be wanting to go back to living in caves, nobody work any more, live *that* way for a while. Used to be a saying about 'Lottery in June, corn be heavy soon.' First thing you know, we'd all be eating stewed chickweed and acorns. There's *always* been a lottery," he added petulantly. "Bad enough to see young Joe Summers up there joking with everybody."

"Some places have already quit lotteries," Mrs. Adams said.

"Nothing but trouble in *that*," Old Man Warner said stoutly. "Pack of young fools."

"Martin." And Bobby Martin watched his father go forward. "Overdyke. ... Percy."

"I wish they'd hurry," Mrs. Dunbar said to her older son. "I wish they'd hurry."

"They're almost through," her son said.

"You get ready to run tell Dad," Mrs. Dunbar said.

Mr. Summers called his own name and then stepped forward precisely and selected a slip from the box. Then he called, "Warner."

"Seventy-seventh year I been in the lottery," Old Man Warner said as he went through the crowd. "Seventy-seventh time."

"Watson." The tall boy came awkwardly through the crowd. Someone said, "Don't be nervous, Jack," and Mr. Summers said, "Take your time, son."

"Zanini."

After that, there was a long pause, a breathless pause, until Mr. Summers, holding his slip of paper in the air, said, "All right, fellows." For a minute, no one moved, and then all the slips of paper were opened. Suddenly, all the women began to speak at once, saying, "Who is it?," "Who's got it?," "Is it the Dunbars?," "Is it the Watsons?" Then the voices began to say, "It's Hutchinson. It's Bill," "Bill Hutchinson's got it."

"Go tell your father," Mrs. Dunbar said to her older son.

People began to look around to see the Hutchinsons. Bill Hutchinson was standing quiet, staring down at the paper in his hand. Suddenly, Tessie Hutchinson shouted to Mr. Summers, "You didn't give him time enough to take any paper he wanted. I saw you. It wasn't fair!"

"Be a good sport, Tessie," Mrs. Delacroix called, and Mrs. Graves said, "All of us took the same chance."

"Shut up, Tessie," Bill Hutchinson said.

"Well, everyone," Mr. Summers said, "that was done pretty fast, and now we've got to be hurrying a little more to get done in time." He consulted his next list. "Bill," he said, "you draw for the Hutchinson family. You got any other households in the Hutchinsons?"

"There's Don and Eva," Mrs. Hutchinson yelled. "Make *them* take their chance!"

"Daughters draw with their husbands' families, Tessie," Mr. Summers said gently. "You know that as well as anyone else."

"It wasn't *fair*," Tessie said.

"I guess not, Joe," Bill Hutchinson said regretfully. "My daughter draws with her husband's family, that's only fair. And I've got no other family except the kids."

"Then, as far as drawing for families is concerned, it's you," Mr. Summers said in explanation, "and as far as drawing for households is concerned, that's you, too. Right?"

"Right," Bill Hutchinson said.

"How many kids, Bill?" Mr. Summers asked formally.

"Three," Bill Hutchinson said. "There's Bill, Jr., and Nancy, and little Dave. And Tessie and me."

"All right, then," Mr. Summers said. "Harry, you got their tickets back?"

Mr. Graves nodded and held up the slips of paper. "Put them in the box, then," Mr. Summers directed. "Take Bill's and put it in."

"I think we ought to start over," Mrs. Hutchinson said, as quietly as she could. "I tell you it wasn't *fair*. You didn't give him time enough to choose. *Every*body saw that."

Mr. Graves had selected the five slips and put them in the box, and he dropped all the papers but those onto the ground, where the breeze caught them and lifted them off.

"Listen, everybody," Mrs. Hutchinson was saying to the people around her.

"Ready, Bill?" Mr. Summers asked, and Bill Hutchinson, with one quick glance around at his wife and children, nodded.

"Remember," Mr. Summers said, "take the slips and keep them folded until each person has taken one. Harry, you help little Dave." Mr. Graves took the hand of the little boy, who came willingly with him up to the box. "Take a paper out of the box, Davy," Mr. Summers said. Davy put his hand into the box and laughed. "Take just *one* paper," Mr. Summers said. "Harry, you hold it for him." Mr. Graves took the child's hand and removed the folded paper from the tight fist and held it while little Dave stood next to him and looked up at him wonderingly.

"Nancy next," Mr. Summers said. Nancy was twelve, and her school friends breathed heavily as she went forward, switching her skirt, and took a slip daintily from the box. "Bill, Jr.," Mr. Summers said, and Billy, his face red and his feet overlarge, nearly knocked the box over as he got a paper out. "Tessie," Mr. Summers said. She hesitated for a minute, looking around defiantly, and then set her lips and went up to the box. She snatched a paper out and held it behind her.

"Bill," Mr. Summers said, and Bill Hutchinson reached into the box and felt around, bringing his hand out at last with the slip of paper in it.

The crowd was quiet. A girl whispered, "I hope it's not Nancy," and the sound of the whisper reached the edges of the crowd.

"It's not the way it used to be," Old Man Warner said clearly. "People ain't the way they used to be."

"All right," Mr. Summers said. "Open the papers. Harry, you open little Dave's."

Mr. Graves opened the slip of paper and there was a general sigh through the crowd as he held it up and everyone could see that it was blank. Nancy and Bill, Jr., opened theirs at the same time, and both beamed and laughed, turning around to the crowd and holding their slips of paper above their heads.

"Tessie," Mr. Summers said. There was a pause, and then Mr. Summers looked at Bill Hutchinson, and Bill unfolded his paper and showed it. It was blank.

"It's Tessie," Mr. Summers said, and his voice was hushed. "Show us her paper, Bill."

Bill Hutchinson went over to his wife and forced the slip of paper out of her hand. It had a black spot on it, the black spot Mr. Summers had made the night before with the heavy pencil in the coal-company office. Bill Hutchinson held it up, and there was a stir in the crowd.

"All right, folks," Mr. Summers said. "Let's finish quickly."

Although the villagers had forgotten the ritual and lost the original black box, they still remembered to use stones. The pile of stones the boys had made earlier was ready; there were stones on the ground with the blowing scraps of paper that had come out of the box. Mrs. Delacroix selected a stone so large she had to pick it up with both hands and turned to Mrs. Dunbar. "Come on," she said. "Hurry up."

Mrs. Dunbar had small stones in both hands, and she said, gasping for breath, "I can't run at all. You'll have to go ahead and I'll catch up with you."

The children had stones already, and someone gave little Davy Hutchinson a few pebbles.

Tessie Hutchinson was in the center of a cleared space by now, and she held her hands out desperately as the villagers moved in on her. "It isn't fair," she said. A stone hit her on the side of the head.

Old Man Warner was saying, "Come on, come on, everyone." Steve Adams was in the front of the crowd of villagers, with Mrs. Graves beside him.

"It isn't fair, it isn't right," Mrs. Hutchinson screamed, and then they were upon her.

Biographical Notes

Shirley Jackson was born in 1919 in San Francisco, where she spent most of her early life. She studied at Syracuse University, New York After graduating with a B.A. degree in 1940, she married the well-known literary critic, Stanley Edgar Hyman, and settled in Vermont.

Here she began to write professionally, finding most of her material in the everyday lives of her neighbours and in the folkways of New England, which particularly fascinated her. Her first novel, The Road Through the Wall, *appeared in 1948, and a collection of short stories entitled* The Lottery *a year later. The title story had caused a literary sensation when first published in* The New Yorker. *She went on to write many other novels and stories, and one of them – a dramatic ghost story – was filmed als* The Haunting. *But it is still mainly "The Lottery" that people associate with her name.*

Shirley Jackson was mother of two daughters and two sons. She died in 1965.

Annotations

32	2	profusely	abundantly, in great numbers
	8	to be through	to be finished
	10	**to assemble**	to gather
	11	**uneasily**	uncomfortably
	12	boisterous	noisy and rough
	13	**reprimand** ['reprɪˌmɑːnd]	angry words (*here*, spoken by a teacher)
	18	**raid**	organized attack (*here*, in order to steal things)
	22	to survey	to watch over
	25	**to fade**	to lose colour

	27	gossip	idle talk about other people
33	1	square dance	traditional American country dance, performed in groups
	2	Halloween	traditional feast on October 31, when children dress up as ghosts, witches, etc.
	3	civic	having to do with the community
	5	a scold	a person who is always scolding, i.e. complaining about s.o.'s behaviour
	15	paraphernalia [ˌpærəfə'neɪljə]	all the equipment needed for s.th.
	27	**stained**	discoloured
	30	**to discard**	to throw away; *here*: to give up
34	1	underfoot	in the way, being walked on
	3	fussing	a lot of (unnecessary) activity
	6	swearing-in	formal ceremony in which s.o. swears to do s.th. correctly
	8	recital [rɪ'saɪtl]	the speaking of some fixed words
		perfunctory	performed as a routine, without interest
	9	tuneless chant	a kind of singing without any melody
		duly	in a proper manner
	10	just so	exactly in this way
	12	to lapse	to go out of use, to be dropped
	18	**interminably**	endlessly
	20	to leave off	to stop (doing s.th.)
	23	clean forgot	*(coll)* quite forgot
	25	to stack	to pile things on top of each other
	30	to crane (one's neck)	to stretch
	32	a farewell	a way of saying goodbye
	35	Missus	(= Mrs) *here*: wife
35	1	**soberly**	seriously
	22	**a hush**	a sudden silence
	29	to disengage o.s.	to break away, to separate
36	9	**gravely**	very seriously
	20	to snort	to make a sound through your nose
	24	chickweed	a wild plant
	25	acorn ['eɪ–]	nut that grows on an oak tree
		petulantly	showing irritation over s.th. trivial
	27	**to quit**	to stop, to give up
	28	stoutly	firmly
37	15	a good sport	s.o. who can play the game
	35	Jr.	Junior; a son named after his father
38	1	to start over	to start again from the beginning
	16	**fist**	closed hand
	19	to switch	*here*: to make s.th. (cloth, etc.) move
	20	daintily	*here*: stiffly and carefully
	23	**defiantly**	showing opposition, resistance
	33	sigh	a letting out of breath, expressing relief
39	1	hushed	quiet
	6	stir	a slight movement

Interpretation and Teaching Notes

Background, Content and Analysis

Of all the practices that human societies are known to have indulged in, none is deplored more than the human sacrifice. Anthropologists may point out its prevalence – from ancient Greece to the Aztecs to more recent occurences in African countries – and explain its ritual significance to the societies in question[1], but the modern mind emotionally rejects it as something unspeakably barbaric, primitive, incomprehensible, foreign to our nature.

Small wonder then that "The Lottery", a story that places such a ritual in a modern American small-town community, should cause the sensation it did when first published in the June 28, 1948 edition of the *New Yorker*. No story they had ever published before had evoked such a response, in the form of a deluge of letters to the editorial offices and the author. The tone of the letters varied from bewildered to downright abusive[2].

Since then the story has acquired the patina of the modern classic, having been widely anthologized (probably the most anthologized story in the U.S.A.). It was adapted for television in 1952, and turned into a one-act play – a favourite for high school groups[3] – a year later. But though now accepted as a literary tour de force, the story has not lost its capacity to shock and disturb. Readers (and even critics) continue to be puzzled as to its meaning.

Shirley Jackson herself was very reluctant to reply to the many requests for explications, and her one published comment[4] on the matter (in a newspaper interview) remains tentative and vague. She does tell us, interestingly enough, that she had her own village in mind as the setting of the story. (This was at the time Bennington, Vermont.) The story idea had come to her while returning from a trip to the grocery store, on a bright June morning.

---

[1] Cf. Sir James George Frazer, "The Scapegoat" in *The Golden Bough*, New York 1951 (particularly relevant to this story are pp. 253–254).

[2] Lenamaja Friedman, *Shirley Jackson*, Twayne's U.S. Authors Series, Boston 1975 (pp. 28, 63–64); see also Shirley Jackson, "Biography of a Story" in *Come Along with Me*, New York: Viking Press, 1968 (pp. 211–224).

[3] Friedman, op. cit. (p. 31).

[4] "Explaining just what I had hoped the story to say is very difficult. I suppose, I hoped, by setting a particularly brutal rite in the present and in my own village to shock the story's readers with a graphic dramatization of the pointless violence and general inhumanity in their own lives." *San Francisco Chronicle*, July 22, 1948: quoted by Friedman, op. cit. (p. 64).

And it is on a bright June morning that the inhabitants of this fictional (or fictionalized) New England village[5] are presented to us. The scene is indeed idyllic, and the holiday atmosphere seems to suggest that the lottery – a traditional annual affair – is a happy, if routine, occasion. Only when the outcome is known, and the real nature of the lottery is revealed at the end of the story, will the reader fully appreciate the horror inherent in the villagers' matter-of-fact attitude.

On a first reading most readers will probably miss the significance of the stones the children are playfully piling up (**32** 14–18, 30). A certain amount of tension evident in the behaviour of the adults (**32** 24–25, 31) will be attributed to the natural excitement of the occasion, which is otherwise comparable to the other community activities mentioned – "the square dances, the teenage club, the Halloween program" (**33** 1–2).

The subsequent description of the paraphernalia and ceremonial details surrounding the lottery serves a multiple function. We learn, for one thing, that the origins of the lottery are lost in the mists of time (**33** 15), and that the present ceremony is a somewhat corrupt version of the original (**33** 30, **34** 7–16). But what is left of the ceremony is fully integrated into the life of the community. Their respect for the tradition goes so far that there is a strong resistance to any further changes such as replacing the splintered and stained old "black box" by a new one (**33** 22–24).

In keeping with the oft-observed male predelection for ceremonial play-acting – of which Mr Summers is a near-caricature – the administration of the lottery is in the hands of a group of men. Typical of the women's more casual, but also more passive attitude to the ceremony is Mrs Hutchinson, who arrives late and quips about having to get her dishes washed. The very typicalness of the characters – we all know somebody like them – serves to underline the surface normality of the situation.

As the first round of the lottery (only for heads of housholds) proceeds, we learn of a certain degree of mild dissent among the villagers as to the sacredness of the tradition. The "liberals" in question are Mr and Mrs Adams, who tentatively remark that some villages have actually given up their lotteries, and the neighbouring village is thinking of doing the same (**36** 18–27). But they are immediately put in their place by the archetypal conservative, Old Man Warner, who has (miraculously) survived seventy-six lotteries. Abandoning the lottery, he points out, would be tantamount to abandoning civilization. (His remark also suggests the possible original significance of the ritual.)

---

[5] As pointed out by John Hagopian and Martin Dolch (*Insight I – Analyses of American Literature*, Frankfurt/Main: Hirschgraben, 1962, p. 129) it could of course be "any small American town in a farm area". But even if we didn't have the author's statement, the atmosphere fits in very well with New England.

Up to this point in the story, tension has been maintained by teasing the readers' curiosity as to the (supposedly pleasant) prize to be won in the lottery. Tessie Hutchinson's reaction when the lot falls on her household (**37** 12–14) is the first sign that there is something really sinister about it. But rising apprehension is likely to be somewhat lulled when the other villagers and even her husband urge her to "be a good sport" and play the game like all the others. Only at the end of the story will the reader fully appreciate what this subordination even of family feeling to the higher demands of the ritual actually means.

And so the ritual takes its course. Tension rises again in the village as the family draw lots. But human feelings are completely out of order – as we are reminded by Old Man Warner's grumpy reaction to a girl's very mild expression of fear for her friend: "People ain't the way they used to be." (**38** 29–30).

But he needn't worry for the villagers' loyalty to the tradition. When it comes to the point they all soberly and matter-of-factly play the roles assigned to them. Tessies hand is pried open by her husband (**39** 1–2), revealing the paper with the black dot. "Let's finish quickly," says the jovial Mr Summers. Stones are picked up and pressed into the hands of even the victim's little son (**39** 16). Then, led by the strange coalition of conservative, liberal, and bureaucrat's wife, "they were upon her".

So what does the story mean? It is certainly not a realistic description of life in a New England village – though it had seemed so, up to a point. Human sacrifice is not, we know, a feature of life in the area, or anywhere else in the U.S.A. or in the civilized world, for that matter. And even if disbelief were to be suspended to the extent that one allows for the survival of such an ancient ritual in an unlikely time and place, there still remains the unexplained "stoicism of the participants and their complete willingness to sacrifice themselves or members of their families"[6]. Undoubtedly an allegory is intended. But an allegory for what?

There is something to be said for leaving the matter open. The author, as we have said, did not want to be pinned down to a narrow interpretation. Lenamaja Friedman, the same critic who finds the villagers' stoicism so irrational, allows that "the lottery may be symbolic of any of a number of social ills that mankind blindly perpetrates"[7].

Cleanth Brooks and Robert Penn Warren quote a number of such social ills, but concentrate on those that share a "scapegoat" element, i.e. the "all-too-human tendency" to seize on a person and visit upon him or her "the cruelties that most of us seem to have dammed up within us"[8]. The rele-

---

[6/7] Friedman, op. cit. (p. 67).
[8] Cleanth Brooks and Robert Penn Warren, *Understanding Fiction*, New York: Meredith Corporation, 1959 (p. 74).

vance of this aspect is underlined by the fact that "scapegoating" is generally recognized to have been a feature of all human sacrifice rituals: the victim takes on all the guilt amassed by the community and appeases the gods by suffering a violent death.

But does the lottery really portray an "all too human tendency" to violence and savagery breaking through the thin crust of civilization? Even those critics who interpret the story in such terms do not fail to notice what is, in effect, a contradiction: namely, that the cruelty involved – far from emerging from the villagers' primitive urges – is actually generated by the tradition[9]. No hatred breaks through, there is no evidence of any human emotion whatsoever. Just a routine, an honoured tradition, a civic duty to be got over before lunch. And there is no doubt that such concepts as tradition and civic duty are important elements of any civilization.

To resolve this apparent contradiction it is not enough to speak vaguely of ambiguity. Multiple meanings should complement, not contradict each other. So how can the lottery both "provide a channel to release repressed cruelties" and at the same time "generate a cruelty not rooted in man's emotional needs at all"?[10] One possible answer would be to distinguish between the individual characters of the story: for some (naturally cruel) individuals it is an outlet, the others are then conditioned by the tradition to follow suit. This possible answer is not, however borne out by the details of the story. The villagers' attitude is remarkably homogeneous. Any resolution must be saught on the community level.

And the evidence of this particular fictive community's behaviour is roughly as follows: that if human nature has anything to do with it, then it is the most natural thing in the world to suppress or suspend one's natural human feelings (love, hate, but also fear and the instinct for self-preservation) in the interests of an evil tradition; or, phrased more speculatively, that it is in our nature as human beings to form communities and develop civilizations (with all their superstitions, religions, group prejudices, ideologies) to which we then gladly sacrifice our more basic human instincts, our capacity for rational thought, and our responsibility.

So, far from opposing and contrasting savagery with civilization, the story demonstrates their identity. Our greatest potential for evil, it is suggested lies in our potential for civilization.

This should not seem too far-fetched a message to any readers in the latter half of the twentieth century – even if previous evidence of cruelty in

---

[9] Cf. Helen Nebeker, "'The Lottery': Symbolic Tour de Force" in *American Literature* 46, 1974 (p. 102): "... the ritual of the lottery, beyond providing a channel to release repressed cruelties, actually serves to *generate* a cruelty not rooted in man's inherent needs at all. Man is not at the mercy of a murky, savage id. He is the victim of unexamined and unchanging traditions ..."

[10] Nebeker, op. cit (p. 102).

high cultures was not enough. If this is what "The Lottery" implies, then it is as good an answer as any to the post-Holocaust questions: How could it happen? How could it happen in such a highly-civilized country? Could it happen elsewhere?

That such questions should have preoccupied Shirley Jackson in 1948 seems more than likely, especially when one considers her marriage to a Jewish literary critic. There are indications that the family was troubled by a certain amount of petty antisemitism in Bennington, which may or may not have to do with their decision to move a year later[11]. In any case, the theme of racial prejudice (against blacks and Jews) has been a recurring one in her writings[12] – as has the nature of human evil.

As a serious answer to a serious question we should perhaps be grateful that the story does contain one optimistic element – namely, the information that "some places have already quit lotteries" (**36** 27).

Recommended Teaching Units (Overview)

I. (Double period) Classroom presentation of first two sections plus **37** 4–26, discussion of content, speculation.
– First section, to **35** 21: preparation for the lottery, intermingled with background information about the community.
– Second section, to **37** 3: the lottery proceeds to point of highest tension. (Focus here on individual characters.)
– **37** 4–26: Tessie Hutchinson's reaction reveals that there is something sinister about the lottery.

II. Home preparation to end of story, discussion of its meaning.

III. After second reading at home, discussion of the technique of foreshadowing.

---

[11] Friedman, op. cit. (pp. 30, 61).
[12] Cf. the *New Yorker* stories "A Fine old Firm" (1944) and "After You, My Dear Alphonse" 1943; she also wrote several articles and editorials in student magazines in support of the NAACP and denouncing racism (Friedman, op. cit. pp. 24–25, 61).

Unit I
The Community and Their Traditions
(Double period)

Notes: If a double period is not available, the material of this unit can be broken up for two separate periods, and the reading of the second section (**35** 22–**37** 3, cf. point 5.) set as homework in preparation for the second period.

For alternatives to the use of the recording see the Teaching Notes to "The Cask of Amontillado", Unit I, introductory note and point 1.

1. The situation (first reading, **32** 1–32)
Before playing the recording of this passage (roughly 3 minutes playing time), the students should be put in the right frame of mind by being asked the most general of comprehension questions in advance: *What is going on here?*

2. Comprehension questions
What is going on?
Where is it going on?
What is the season?
What kind of a community is it?
What are we told about the men? – the women? – the children?
What names are mentioned?
Describe the atmosphere.
The students should be allowed to refer to their books to clear up any points they have not understood. Before going on, they could be asked: *What have you still not understood? What would you like to know?* Caution: The matter of the stones (**32** 14–18, 30) should only be touched on if raised by the students themselves, and glossed over as far as possible.

3. Reading/listening to end of first section (**33** 1–**35** 21, playing time roughly 8 minutes).

4. Background of the lottery (comprehension and discussion)
Who is responsible for running the lottery?
How is it organized?
How old is the tradition?
What has changed over the years?
How important does the lottery seem to be in the life of the community?
Is the community unique in having this tradition?
The last question will force the students to refer back to the beginning of the story (**32** 4–6). Even in dealing with the others, they should be allowed to constantly refer to the text.

5. Second section, first reading (**35** 22–**37** 3, playing time 5 minutes)
At this stage, the main purpose of proceeding with the story will be to find out what this mysterious lottery is all about. However, the students should be asked in addition to pay particular attention to one character or family. They can be allowed to choose the characters that interest them most, but the teacher should ensure that somebody at least is concentrating on each family/person already mentioned – and somebody watching out for people not yet mentioned.

6. Individuals and their attitudes (comprehension and discussion)
What differences exist among the villagers as regards their attitude to the lottery?
The students should report here on the attitudes of the characters they have chosen to pay particular attention to. The main discussion point will be the dispute between Old Man Warner (the archetypal "traditionalist") and the Adams family ("progressives").

7. General feeling about the lottery (comprehension and discussion)
After reading/listening to this section, do you know any more about the nature of the lottery?
What seems to be the mood of the crowd? Where is it evident?
What do you think the mood is when they reach the name "Zanini"?

8. The beginning of the next section (**37** 4–26, playing time 2 minutes) should be read/listened to as preparation for the next point.

9. The nature of the lottery (speculation)
The class can here be divided into groups of 3–5 students, and each group asked to pool their various speculations as to what the lottery is about, and put down their conclusions in writing. Books should not be used – to prevent cheating; photocopies with the last two pages missing can be made available if desired. (If any students have already read to the end, they should be made group leaders or observers, with the job of taking notes about the progress of their classmates.)

   The conclusions the various groups have come to should then be compared and discussed. The teacher should play a minimal role at this stage, and avoid commenting on the students' speculation – even if some students come close to drawing the correct conclusions. (There is usually a strong resistance to this conclusion, "No, it can't be!" being a typical reaction.)

Homework: Read to the end.

Unit II
The Ending: What Does It Mean?

1. Reactions to the ending
As many individual students as possible should be given the opportunity to describe the effect the revelation of the nature of the lottery had on them: surprise, shock, horror, confirmation of worst fears, sympathy, disgust, dislike, etc.

2. Discussion of its effect
Why do you feel like this?
Why does the ending have such a strong effect?
What has the setting got to do with the shock effect of the ending?
Which questions are most appropriate will depend on the accounts of the effect given by the students under point 1. In any case a discussion should ensue of the way the horror is magnified by being embedded in a setting of apparently normal everyday life.

3. Realism or allegory?
Is the author telling us that this kind of behaviour is to be expected in a rural areas of the U.S.A.?
If not, what is she telling us?
It should emerge that some form of allegory is intended, though precisely what it signifies will probably be in dispute. The general human traits depicted in the story should be enough to rule out any restriction of its message to the U.S.A. Most likely the students will – correctly – conclude that the message is something about the human potential for cruelty.

4. The villagers' motivation
How naturally cruel are the villagers?
Or are they motivated by some strong emotion, such as hate or fear?
Do they need a scapegoat? If so, for what?
Is this their savage nature breaking through the crust of civilization?
Or are they only too civilized and law-abiding, with too much respect for tradition?
Most of these questions should have emerged from the discussion under the previous point. It may help at this stage to listen to the remainder of the recording (**37** 27–**39** 25, playing time 6 minutes), concentrating this time on the relationship between the villagers' individual human feelings and their behaviour. The discrepancies should be obvious.

5. Conclusions
No interpretation should be forced on the students. It may remain in dispute whether Shirley Jackson is telling us something about the "scapegoating" mechanism in human society, or about blind obedience to tradition/

authority, or both. But the relevance of her shocking allegory should not be overlooked. One final question should be raised, if it has not already been raised in the course of this unit:
Can you find any example in recent history of savage behaviour in a highly-civilized society?

Homework: Re-read the whole story.

Unit III
The Technique of Foreshadowing

1. The first page
When re-reading the first page, what things did you notice that you had overlooked the first time round?
Why had you overlooked them?
It is of course possible that some readers had been wondering about the significance of the stones – but even if so, they will have brushed such thoughts aside. The author has given some very significant hints, but at the same time made sure that they are crowded out by other seemingly more interesting details. As well as the reference to the stones there are two suggestions of tension in the behaviour of the villagers: **32** 11, 24–25.

2. Other hints
Where else in the story can you find hints as to the sinister nature of the lottery?
Some may now find something sinister in the fact that they use a "black box" (**33** 19) for the lottery. Otherwise the next hints are the unexplained references to some villagers' nervousness: **35** 17, 31–32; **36** 12; **37** 1, 4; and then the definitive evidence (**37** 14) that winning the lottery is something very undesirable indeed. The Adams–Warner dispute will also be seen in a new light, in the knowledge that lotteries are something that enlightened, progressive people would want to give up.

3. Effect of foreshadowing
Was the surprise ending an unfair trick – or should you have guessed?
Open discussion. Very few will have correctly interpreted the hints, but they were there. The author has successfully exploited our habitual ways of thinking, and our resistance to thinking the seemingly unthinkable.

Roald Dahl

The Landlady

Billy Weaver had travelled down from London on the slow afternoon train, with a change at Swindon on the way, and by the time he got to Bath it was about nine o'clock in the evening and the moon was coming up out of a clear starry sky over the houses opposite the station entrance. But the air was deadly cold and the wind was like a flat blade of ice on his cheeks.

"Excuse me," he said, "but is there a fairly cheap hotel not too far away from here?"

"Try The Bell and Dragon," the porter answered, pointing down the road. "They might take you in. It's about a quarter of a mile along on the other side."

Billy thanked him and picked up his suitcase and set out to walk the quarter-mile to The Bell and Dragon. He had never been to Bath before. He didn't know anyone who lived there. But Mr Greenslade at the Head Office in London had told him it was a splendid city. "Find your own lodgings," he had said, "and then go along and report to the Branch Manager as soon as you've got yourself settled."

Billy was seventeen years old. He was wearing a new navy-blue overcoat, a new brown trilby hat, and a new brown suit, and he was feeling fine. He walked briskly down the street. He was trying to do everything briskly these days. Briskness, he had decided, was *the* one common characteristic of all successful businessmen. The big shots up at Head Office were absolutely fantastically brisk all the time. They were amazing.

There were no shops on this wide street that he was walking along, only a line of tall houses on each side, all of them identical. They had porches and pillars and four or five steps going up to their front doors, and it was obvious that once upon a time they had been very swanky residences. But now, even in the darkness, he could see that the paint was peeling from the woodwork on their doors and windows, and that the handsome white façades were cracked and blotchy from neglect.

Suddenly, in a downstairs window that was brilliantly illuminated by a street-lamp not six yards away, Billy caught sight of a printed notice propped up against the glass in one of the upper panes. It said BED AND BREAKFAST.

There was a vase of pussy willows, tall and beautiful, standing just underneath the notice.

He stopped walking. He moved a bit closer. Green curtains (some sort of velvety material) were hanging down on either side of the window. The pussy willows looked wonderful beside them. He went right up and peered through the glass into the room, and the first thing he saw was a bright fire burning in the hearth. On the carpet in front of the fire, a pretty little dachshund was curled up asleep with its nose tucked into its belly. The room itself, so far as he could see in the half-darkness, was filled with pleasant furniture. There was a baby-grand piano and a big sofa and several plump armchairs; and in one corner he spotted a large parrot in a cage. Animals were usually a good sign in a place like this, Billy told himself; and all in all, it looked to him as though it would be a pretty decent house to stay in. Certainly it would be more comfortable than The Bell and Dragon.

On the other hand, a pub would be more congenial than a boarding-house. There would be beer and darts in the evenings, and lots of people to talk to, and it would probably be a good bit cheaper, too. He had stayed a couple of nights in a pub once before and he had liked it. He had never stayed in any boarding-houses, and, to be perfectly honest, he was a tiny bit frightened of them. The name itself conjured up images of watery cabbage, rapacious landladies, and a powerful smell of kippers in the living-room.

After dithering about like this in the cold for two or three minutes, Billy decided that he would walk on and take a look at The Bell and Dragon before making up his mind. He turned to go.

And now a queer thing happened to him. He was in the act of stepping back and turning away from the window when all at once his eye was caught and held in the most peculiar manner by the small notice that was there. BED AND BREAKFAST, it said. BED AND BREAKFAST, BED AND BREAKFAST, BED AND BREAKFAST. Each word was like a large black eye staring at him through the glass, holding him, compelling him, forcing him to stay where he was and not to walk away from that house, and the next thing he knew, he was actually moving across from the window to the front door of the house, climbing the steps that led up to it, and reaching for the bell.

He pressed the bell. Far away in a back room he heard it ringing, and then *at once* – it must have been at once because he hadn't even had time to take his finger from the bell-button – the door swung open and a woman was standing there.

Normally you ring the bell and you have at least a half-minute's wait before the door opens. But this dame was like a jack-in-the-box. He pressed the bell – and out she popped! It made him jump.

She was about forty-five or fifty years old, and the moment she saw him, she gave him a warm welcoming smile.

"*Please* come in," she said pleasantly. She stepped aside, holding the door wide open, and Billy found himself automatically starting forward into the house. The compulsion or, more accurately, the desire to follow after her into that house was extraordinarily strong.

"I saw the notice in the window," he said, holding himself back.

"Yes, I know."

"I was wondering about a room."

"It's *all* ready for you, my dear," she said. She had a round pink face and very gentle blue eyes.

"I was on my way to The Bell and Dragon," Billy told her. "But the notice in your window just happened to catch my eye."

"My dear boy," she said, "why don't you come in out of the cold?"

"How much do you charge?"

"Five and sixpence a night, including breakfast."

It was fantastically cheap. It was less than half of what he had been willing to pay.

"If that is too much," she added, "then perhaps I can reduce it just a tiny bit. Do you desire an egg for breakfast? Eggs are expensive at the moment. It would be sixpence less without the egg."

"Five and sixpence is fine," he answered. "I should like very much to stay here."

"I knew you would. Do come in."

She seemed terribly nice. She looked exactly like the mother of one's best school-friend welcoming one into the house to stay for the Christmas holidays. Billy took off his hat, and stepped over the threshold.

"Just hang it there," she said, "and let me help you with your coat."

There were no other hats or coats in the hall. There were no umbrellas, no walking-sticks – nothing.

"We have it *all* to ourselves," she said, smiling at him over her shoulder as she led the way upstairs. "You see, it isn't very often I have the pleasure of taking a visitor into my little nest."

The old girl is slightly dotty, Billy told himself. But at five and sixpence a night, who gives a damn about that? "I should've thought you'd be simply swamped with applicants," he said politely.

"Oh, I am, my dear, I am, of course I am. But the trouble is that I'm inclined to be just a teeny weeny bit choosy and particular – if you see what I mean."

"Ah, yes."

"But I'm always ready. Everything is always ready day and night in this house just on the off-chance that an acceptable young gentleman will come along. And it is such a pleasure, my dear, such a very great pleasure when now and again I open the door and I see someone standing there who is just *exactly* right." She was half-way up the stairs, and she paused with one hand on the stair-rail, turning her head and smiling down at him with pale lips. "Like you," she added, and her blue eyes travelled slowly all the way down the length of Billy's body, to his feet, and then up again.

On the first-floor landing she said to him, "This floor is mine."

They climbed up a second flight. "And this one is *all* yours," she said. "Here's your room. I do hope you'll like it." She took him into a small but charming front bedroom, switching on the light as she went in.

"The morning sun comes right in the window, Mr Perkins. It *is* Mr Perkins, isn't it?"

"No," he said. "It's Weaver."

"Mr Weaver. How nice. I've put a water-bottle between the sheets to air them out, Mr Weaver. It's such a comfort to have a hot water-bottle in a strange bed with clean sheets, don't you agree? And you may light the gas fire at any time if you feel chilly."

"Thank you," Billy said. "Thank you ever so much." He noticed that the bedspread had been taken off the bed, and that the bedclothes had been neatly turned back on one side, all ready for someone to get in.

"I'm so glad you appeared," she said, looking earnestly into his face. "I was beginning to get worried."

"That's all right," Billy answered brightly. "You mustn't worry about me." He put his suitcase on the chair and started to open it.

"And what about supper, my dear? Did you manage to get anything to eat before you came here?"

"I'm not a bit hungry, thank you," he said. "I think I'll just go to bed as soon as possible because tomorrow I've got to get up rather early and report to the office."

"Very well, then. I'll leave you now so that you can unpack. But before you go to bed, would you be kind enough to pop into the sitting-room on the ground floor and sign the book? Everyone has to do that because it's the law of the land, and we don't want to go breaking any laws at *this* stage in the proceedings, do we?" She gave him a little wave of the hand and went quickly out of the room and closed the door.

Now, the fact that his landlady appeared to be slightly off her rocker didn't worry Billy in the least. After all, she was not only harmless – there was no question about that – but she was also quite obviously a kind and generous soul. He guessed that she had probably lost a son in the war, or something like that, and had never got over it.

So a few minutes later, after unpacking his suitcase and washing his hands, he trotted downstairs to the ground floor and entered the living-room. His landlady wasn't there, but the fire was glowing in the hearth, and the little dachshund was still sleeping in front of it. The room was wonderfully warm and cosy. I'm a lucky fellow, he thought, rubbing his hands. This is a bit of all right.

He found the guest-book lying open on the piano, so he took out his pen and wrote down his name and address. There were only two other entries above his on the page, and, as one always does with guest-books, he started to read them. One was a Christopher Mulholland from Cardiff. The other was Gregory W. Temple from Bristol.

That's funny, he thought suddenly. Christopher Mulholland. It rings a bell.

Now where on earth had he heard that rather unusual name before?

Was he a boy at school? No. Was it one of his sister's numerous young men, perhaps, or a friend of his father's? No, no, it wasn't any of those. He glanced down again at the book.

Christopher Mulholland   *231 Cathedral Road, Cardiff*

Gregory W. Temple   *27 Sycamore Drive, Bristol*

As a matter of fact, now he came to think of it, he wasn't at all sure that the second name didn't have almost as much of a familiar ring about it as the first.

"Gregory Temple?" he said aloud, searching his memory. "Christopher Mulholland? ..."

"Such charming boys," a voice behind him answered, and he turned and saw his landlady sailing into the room with a large silver tea-tray in her hands. She was holding it well out in front of her, and rather high up, as though the tray were a pair of reins on a frisky horse.

"They sound somehow familiar," he said.

"They do? How interesting."

"I'm almost positive I've heard those names before somewhere. Isn't that queer? Maybe it was in the newspapers. They weren't famous in any way, were they? I mean famous cricketers or footballers or something like that?"

"Famous," she said, setting the tea-tray down on the low table in front of the sofa. "Oh no, I don't think they were famous. But they were extraordinarily handsome, both of them, I can promise you that. They were tall and young and handsome, my dear, just exactly like you."

Once more, Billy glanced down at the book. "Look here," he said, noticing the dates. "This last entry is over two years old."

"It is?"

"Yes, indeed. And Christopher Mulholland's is nearly a year before that – more than *three years* ago."

"Dear me," she said, shaking her head and heaving a dainty little sigh. "I would never have thought it. How time does fly away from us all, doesn't it, Mr Wilkins?"

"It's Weaver," Billy said. "W-e-a-v-e-r."

"Oh, of course it is!" she cried, sitting down on the sofa. "How silly of me. I do apologize. In one ear and out the other, that's me, Mr Weaver."

"You know something?" Billy said. "Something that's really quite extraordinary about all this?"

"No, dear, I don't."

"Well, you see – both of these names, Mulholland and Temple, I not only seem to remember each one of them separately, so to speak, but somehow or other, in some peculiar way, they both appear to be sort of connected together as well. As though they were both famous for the same sort of thing, if you see what I mean – like ... well ... like Dempsey and Tunney, for example, or Churchill and Roosevelt."

"How amusing," she said. "But come over here now, dear, and sit down beside me on the sofa and I'll give you a nice cup of tea and a ginger biscuit before you go to bed."

"You really shouldn't bother," Billy said. "I didn't mean you to do anything like that." He stood by the piano, watching her as she fussed about with the cups and saucers. He noticed that she had small, white, quickly moving hands, and red finger-nails.

"I'm almost positive it was in the newspapers I saw them," Billy said. "I'll think of it in a second. I'm sure I will."

There is nothing more tantalizing than a thing like this which lingers just outside the borders of one's memory. He hated to give up.

"Now wait a minute," he said. "Wait just a minute. Mulholland ... Christopher Mulholland ... wasn't *that* the name of the Eton schoolboy who was on a walking-tour through the West Country, and then all of a sudden ..."

"Milk?" she said. "And sugar?"

"Yes, please. And then all of a sudden ..."

"Eton schoolboy?" she said. "Oh no, my dear, that can't possibly be right because *my* Mr Mulholland was certainly not an Eton schoolboy when he came to me. He was a Cambridge undergraduate. Come over here now and sit next to me and warm yourself in front of this lovely fire. Come on. Your

75

tea's all ready for you." She patted the empty place beside her on the sofa, and she sat there smiling at Billy and waiting for him to come over.

He crossed the room slowly, and sat down on the edge of the sofa. She placed his teacup on the table in front of him.

"*There* we are," she said. "How nice and cosy this is, isn't it?"

Billy started sipping his tea. She did the same. For half a minute or so, neither of them spoke. But Billy knew that she was looking at him. Her body was half-turned towards him, and he could feel her eyes resting on his face, watching him over the rim of her teacup. Now and again, he caught a whiff of a peculiar smell that seemed to emanate directly from her person. It was not in the least unpleasant, and it reminded him – well, he wasn't quite sure what it reminded him of. Pickled walnuts? New leather? Or was it the corridors of a hospital?

"Mr Mulholland was a great one for his tea," she said at length. "Never in my life have I seen anyone drink as much tea as dear, sweet Mr Mulholland."

"I suppose he left fairly recently," Billy said. He was still puzzling his head about the two names. He was positive now that he had seen them in the newspapers – in the headlines.

"Left?" she said, arching her brows. "But my dear boy, he never left. He's still here. Mr Temple is also here. They're on the third floor, both of them together."

Billy set down his cup slowly on the table, and stared at his landlady. She smiled back at him, and then she put out one of her white hands and patted him comfortingly on the knee. "How old are you, my dear?" she asked.

"Seventeen."

"Seventeen!" she cried. "Oh, it's the perfect age! Mr Mulholland was also seventeen. But I think he was a trifle shorter than you are, in fact I'm sure he was, and his teeth weren't *quite* so white. You have the most beautiful teeth, Mr Weaver, did you know that?"

"They're not as good as they look," Billy said. "They've got simply masses of fillings in them at the back."

"Mr Temple, of course, was a little older," she said, ignoring his remark. "He was actually twenty-eight. And yet I never would have guessed it if he hadn't told me, never in my whole life. There wasn't a *blemish* on his body."

"A what?" Billy said.

"His skin was *just* like a baby's."

There was a pause. Billy picked up his teacup and took another sip of his tea, then he set it down again gently in its saucer. He waited for her to say something else, but she seemed to have lapsed into another of her silences.

He sat there staring straight ahead of him into the far corner of the room, biting his lower lip.

"That parrot," he said at last. "You know something? It had me completely fooled when I first saw it through the window from the street. I could have sworn it was alive."

"Alas, no longer."

"It's most terribly clever the way it's been done," he said. "It doesn't look in the least bit dead. Who did it?"

"I did."

"*You* did?"

"Of course," she said. "And have you met my little Basil as well?" She nodded towards the dachshund curled up so comfortably in front of the fire. Billy looked at it. And suddenly, he realized that this animal had all the time been just as silent and motionless as the parrot. He put out a hand and touched it gently on the top of its back. The back was hard and cold, and when he pushed the hair to one side with his fingers, he could see the skin underneath, greyish-black and dry and perfectly preserved.

"Good gracious me," he said. "How absolutely fascinating." He turned away from the dog and stared with deep admiration at the little woman beside him on the sofa. "It must be most awfully difficult to do a thing like that."

"Not in the least," she said. "I stuff *all* my little pets myself when they pass away. Will you have another cup of tea?"

"No, thank you," Billy said. The tea tasted faintly of bitter almonds, and he didn't much care for it.

"You did sign the book, didn't you?"

"Oh, yes."

"That's good. Because later on, if I happen to forget what you were called, then I can always come down here and look it up. I still do that almost every day with Mr Mulholland and Mr ... Mr ..."

"Temple," Billy said. "Gregory Temple. Excuse my asking, but haven't there been *any* other guests here except them in the last two or three years?"

Holding her teacup high in one hand, inclining her head slightly to the left, she looked up at him out of the corners of her eyes and gave him another gentle little smile.

"No, my dear," she said. "Only you."

Biographical Notes

Though his parents were Norwegian, Roald Dahl was born in South Wales in 1916. After taking part in an expedition to explore the interior of Newfoundland, he worked for Shell Oil in East Africa. Then World War II broke out, and he became a fighter pilot in the Royal Air Force. He was seriously injured in the Libyan Desert, but recovered to fight again in Greece and Syria. In 1942 he was sent to Washington as Assistant Air Attaché, and it was there that he began to write stories.

His first stories – all inspired by his war experiences – were published in various American magazines, and later reprinted in book form as Over to You *(1945). Several other collections followed, including* Kiss Kiss *(1959), from which this story is taken.*

Dahl, The Landlady

Roald Dahl soon acquired a considerable reputation for the sly humour of his stories, their unexpected twists, and very often (as in "The Landlady"), a touch of the macabre. His books became best-sellers in many countries. Several of his stories were televised with great success in Britain. He has also been successful as a writer of children's books and of film screenplays. He is married, with four children, and lives in Buckinghamshire.

Annotations

42		landlady	a woman who takes paying guests or rents rooms
	5	deadly	*here:* very, extremely
		blade	part of a knife that cuts
	14	lodgings	a place to stay
	15	to report to	to present oneself when starting work
	18	trilby hat	a hat made of soft felt
	19	brisk	quick, lively, as if one is in a hurry
	20	the one common characteristic	the one thing they had in common
	21	big shot	*(coll.)* important person
	24	**porch**	roofed area in front of a door
	25	pillar	a tall, usually round stone structure (holding up a roof, for example)
	26	swanky	*(coll.)* very fine, typical of the rich
	29	blotchy	with marks, unevenly coloured
		neglect	lack of care
	31	to prop up	to hold up
43	1	pussy willow	a plant with soft "hair"
	4	velvet	like velvet *(Samt)*
	5	to peer	to look with difficulty
	7	hearth [ɑ:]	place for an open fire
		dachshund ['dækshʊnd]	a small dog with short legs
	8	curled up	rolled together
	10	baby-grand piano	the smallest kind of grand piano (i.e. not the upright kind)
		plump	fat
	15	congenial [kən'dʒi:njəl]	pleasant
		boarding-house	private house that accepts paying guests
	20	to conjure up ['kʌndʒə]	to bring to mind
		rapacious [rə'peɪʃəs]	greedy, always wanting money
	21	kipper	smoked herring
	22	to dither	to keep changing one's mind
	39	jack-in-the-box	a puppet that springs out of a box when the box is opened
44	5	**compulsion**	feeling of being compelled, of having to do s.th.
	16	five and sixpence	i.e. five and a half shillings; a shilling is the equivalent of five (new) pence, not allowing for inflation

	27	**threshold**	border (in doorway) between inside and outside
	34	dotty	*(coll.)* mad.
	36	to be swamped with applicants	to have too many people applying (for rooms)
	38	teeny weeny	*(coll.)* little, small
		choosy, particular	hard to please
45	2	off-chance	slight possibility
	19	**chilly**	cold
	21	bedspread	a day cover for a bed
	35	at this stage in the proceedings	*(formal)* at this point
	38	off one's rocker	*(coll.)* mad
46	7	a bit of all right	*(coll.)* very fine
	14	to ring a bell	to sound familiar
	27	reins [reɪnz]	leather straps for holding and controlling a horse
		frisky	lively
47	6	to heave a sigh	to let out a deep breath (as a sign of sadness, etc.)
		dainty	*here:* ladylike
	19	Dempsey, Tunney	famous American boxers
	22	ginger [ˈdʒɪndʒə]	a spice used in cakes and biscuits *(Ingwer)*
	30	tantalizing	frustrating (because you cannot reach or get s.th.)
		to linger [ŋg]	to stay
	39	undergraduate	university student (who has not yet graduated)
48	10	to emanate [ˈemәneɪt]	to come from a source
	19	to arch one's brows	to raise one's eyebrows
	27	a trifle	a bit
	34	blemish [ˈblemɪʃ]	mark, visible fault
	40	to lapse into	to fall back into
49	23	almond [ˈɑːmənd]	a kind of white nut *(Mandel)*
	32	to incline	to bend, to tilt

Interpretation and Teaching Notes

Background, Content and Analysis

The huge popularity of Roald Dahl's *Tales of the Unexpected* – both the Penguin collections and the TV series of the same name – might give the impression that he invented the surprise genre. Not so. But our anthology would indeed be incomplete without him. Not just because of his undoubted mastery of all aspects of suspense, surprise and shock, but because of his special trade mark, the sly humour by which even the most macabre outcome is rendered palatable and even enjoyable. All of this and more is evident in "The Landlady".

The story begins with a straightforward description of a very ordinary occurrence – the arrival of a young man (Billy) in the provincial town (Bath, near Bristol in the west of England) where he is to take up his first job the following day. The first touch of humour is where we see (**42** 17–22) that seventeen-year-old Billy, with his "new brown trilby hat" and deliberately "brisk" manner is trying hard to live up to the image of the "successful businessman".

This is also the point where the reader's double perspective becomes evident – something which is very important for the development of suspense as the story proceeds. We share Billy's thoughts and perceptions, but we are free to draw our own conclusions. For the moment, however, Billy's observations are all we need. He is a wide-awake young man, taking in all the details of his surroundings as he proceeds to look for lodgings in the unfamiliar town.

Most readers will have a sympathetic understanding for Billy's indecision as he dithers between going on to the inn he has been directed to and inquiring at the Bed and Breakfast place he passes on the way. The place does seem attractive, but not quite attractive enough to overcome his (understandable) dislike of boarding houses (**43** 18–21).

"And now a queer thing happened" (**43** 25). Here, a touch of the supernatural enters this seemingly ordinary story. Just about to walk away, Billy is strangely drawn to the B&B sign, and feels compelled to ring the bell. The door opens as if someone has been waiting for him – a middle-aged lady with a "welcoming smile" (**44** 2). Together with the strange compulsion that Billy was overcome by, this welcome has a strong touch of the fairy tale to it – of "Hansel and Gretel", to be precise. An appropriate allusion, as it turns out.

This is the only touch of the supernatural in the story, and it remains unexplained to the end. In any case its effect is to warn the reader that just about anything can happen from then on.

Needless to say Billy decides to stay. He finds it strange that there are no other guests, and that the landlady should be fussing over him like a long lost son (his explanation, as it happens, **46** 1), "but at five and sixpence a night, who gives a damn about that?" (**44** 34–35). Besides, he seems to quite enjoy being fussed over (**44** 25–27, **45** 40, **46** 6–8).

The second half of the story consists of an accumulation of clues that something is seriously amiss, accompanied by rising suspense. The suspense is heightened by the growing discrepancy between Billy's and the reader's level of awareness. With Billy willing to turn a blind eye to the landlady's "dottiness", the reader will have become far more efficient at reading the signs. Sooner or later it dawns on us what fate lies in store for the hero, but we are unable to warn him.

The first of these signs is the guest book, with its two vaguely familiar names (**46** 10–**47** 34). Just when Billy seems to have remembered where he heard these names before, he is distracted by the landlady's offer of a cup of tea – leaving the reader to mentally complete what he was going to say: "... when they disappeared."

Then comes the smell which he is unable to identify (**48** 9–13) at first. Again his thoughts are interrupted by the landlady's chatter – this time including the weird statement that his two predecessors "never left" (**48** 19), and some macabre remarks about Billy's and their ages and physical features.

And in case any readers have not yet understood in what sense Mr Temple and Mr Mulholland are "on the third floor, both of them together" (**48** 20–21), there follows the revelation that the parrot and the dog that had made the house seem so cosy when he first looked through the window (**43** 7–13) are both stuffed: "I stuff all my little pets myself when they pass away. Will you have another cup of tea?" (**49** 21–22).

But the tea tastes of bitter almonds – to any detective story reader a sure sign that it contains cyanide. It is too late. But in a final macabre touch, the small talk goes on, with the landlady assuring Billy of his privileged position: there have indeed been no other guests since then – "only you".

Recommended Teaching Units (Overview)

I. (Double period) Presentation of whole story in class; discussion and speculation at various points in the story.

II. After re-reading at home, discussion of the technique of foreshadowing.

Unit I
Suspense and Foreboding
(Double period)

Note: Though the use of the recording is not essential, it is strongly recommended as a way of maintaining the pace and upholding suspense. Should a double period not be available, this first reading may be spread over two separate periods, with the option of setting the reading of the second half of the story as homework. The playing times given here are approximate.

1. Lines **42** 1–22 (playing time 2 minutes, to be repeated after point a) if necessary)
a) Comprehension questions:
Who is Billy Weaver?
How old is he?
Where has he travelled from?
Where has he arrived?
What does he look for on arrival?
What situation is he in?
How is he dressed? Why?
b) Humour, narrative technique and point of view:
Whose thoughts and feelings are we allowed to share?
What is your attitude to Billy?
– Can you sympathize with him?
– Do you fully identify with him?
– Or are you laughing at him?
The point touched on here is that the humour evident in the paragraph **42** 17–22 creates a certain distance – sympathy and understanding for the protagonist, but not full identification.
However, this need not be made explicit at this stage.

2. Lines **42** 23–**43** 24 (playing time 2 minutes)
What is The Bell and Dragon?
Why does Billy want to go there?
Describe the street he walks down.
Why does he stop?
What does he see when he looks closer?
What impression does it make on him?
What does he think of the animals?
Why does he not go in?
Do you agree that this is the right decision?

3. Lines **43** 25–**46** 2 (playing time 7 minutes)
a) Short summary of the action by the students

b) Discussion points:
What "queer thing happened to him" before he could leave?
– Can you explain it?
– What effect does it have on you?
What is your impression of the landlady?
– Is it the same as Billy's?
– Is there anything you find particularly strange?
If you were in Billy's situation, would you have stayed?
– Why? / Why not?

4. Lines **46** 3–36 (playing time 3 minutes)
What is surprising to Billy about the names in the guest book?
What possible explanations does he think of?
Can you think of any more?

5. Lines **47** 1–**48** 5 (playing time 3 minutes)
What does Billy begin to remember about the two names?
What do you think he was going to say when interrupted? (Repeat **47** 32–34)
How does the landlady deal with his speculation?
What do you think is going to happen?

6. Lines **48** 6–**49** 35, to end (playing time – 5 minutes)
Well, what is the explanation? What has happened to Mulholland and Temple?
What has happened to Billy?
When did you begin to guess?
When were you sure?
Answers to the last two questions will vary, especially as regards which of the clues in this final section have been decisive.

Homework: Read the whole story, and pick out/mark all the clues as to the landlady's real intentions.

Unit II
Reading the Signs

Note: A number of the points dealt with here may have been touched upon in the previous unit – depending on what the students did or did not notice in the course of their first confrontation with the story. It is up to the teacher to decide how much emphasis still needs to be given to such points.

1. Clues and other warning signs (discussion of homework)
Did you find any clue or warning sign in the first page?
Answer either "No" or – possibly – the humorous reference to Billy's youth and naïveté (**42** 17–22), which indirectly signals that the reader may be

aware of more than Billy is.
What clues did you find?
The following passages should be discussed in the sequence in which they are brought up by the students. Omissions can be dealt with in a second round.

43 18–21: a rather negative picture of boarding-houses in general
43 25–37, **44** 3–6: the strange "compulsion" – a touch of the supernatural, an unexplained mystery, hint of a fairy-tale
43 38–40: the landlady has been waiting for him – strange indeed
44 1ff: the landlady's strangely effusive behaviour (suggestion of wicked witch in a fairy tale)?
44 16–24: the room is too cheap – what's wrong with it?
44 29–33: no other guests
45 7–8: something strange in the way she looks at Billy
45 23–24: another sign that she has been expecting him
45 34–36: a hint of a more serious kind of law-breaking at a later stage?
46 12–23, 28–32: names in guest book sound familiar (possible to guess at this point that they were murder victims, though the evidence is as yet slight)
47 15–20: names connected in some way
47 32–34: Billy remembers where he heard one of the names
47 35–40: the landlady interrupts Billy before he can finish what is presumably a reference to an unexplained crime
48 6–9: awkward silence
48 9–13: strange smell – a foreshadowing of the "bitter almonds" smell he identifies later (see below)
48 19–21: Mulholland and Temple "still here"
48 26–37: the landlady's strange comparisons of the physical attributes of the three boys
48 38–**49** 2: another awkward silence – Billy feels something is wrong, but cannot identify it
49 3–17, 21–22: revelation that the landlady's pets are all dead and stuffed
49 23–24: strange smell identified – suggests cyanide in his tea
49 25–35: confirmation that Billy is to suffer the same fate as all the landlady's other "pets"

2. Billy and the reader – discrepancy in awareness
Billy seems to be an intelligent and observant boy in most respects. Why does he not read the signs correctly and save himself?
The more obvious signs should be taken in turn and Billy's reactions examined.
44 17–35: His desire for a bargain, together with the landlady's niceness, overrules the strangeness of the situation. Besides, he does seem to be at the mercy of some strange "compulsion".

85

44 34, **45** 38–**46** 2: He attributes the landlady's strange behaviour to being slightly "dotty" in a harmless way, and even finds a rational explanation for this. It seems he doesn't want to imagine anything worse – which would, after all, be rather unlikely.

47 32–**48** 9: Billy is disturbed by the landlady's interruptions, and must have some suspicion what this means. But he probably decides it is just too fantastic.

49 7–20: Billy does not (though we feel he should) link the revelation about the stuffed pets to the mystery of the previous guests. Instead he expresses astonishment and what seems to be genuine admiration for her skill.

49 23–24: The significance of the strange taste of the tea escapes him – maybe he hasn't read many murder mysteries.

3. Evaluation
Did you like this story?
Would you regard it as a horror story? Why? / Why not?
Personal reactions called for. It will probably emerge that the humour and the fairy-tale elements have taken the sting out of the horror.

Arthur C. Clarke

History Lesson

No one could remember when the tribe had begun its long journey. The land of great rolling plains that had been its first home was now no more than a half-forgotten dream.

For many years Shann and his people had been fleeing through a country of low hills and sparkling lakes, and now the mountains lay ahead. This summer they must cross them to the southern lands. There was little time to lose. The white terror that had come down from the Poles, grinding continents to dust and freezing the very air before it, was less than a day's march behind.

Shann wondered if the glaciers could climb the mountains ahead, and within his heart he dared to kindle a little flame of hope. This might prove a barrier against which even the remorseless ice would batter in vain. In the southern lands of which the legends spoke, his people might find refuge at last.

It took weeks to discover a pass through which the tribe and the animals could travel. When midsummer came, they had camped in a lonely valley where the air was thin and the stars shone with a brilliance no one had ever seen before.

The summer was waning when Shann took his two sons and went ahead to explore the way. For three days they climbed, and for three nights slept as best they could on the freezing rocks, and on the fourth morning there was nothing ahead but a gentle rise to a cairn of gray stones built by other travelers, centuries ago.

Shann felt himself trembling, and not with cold, as they walked toward the little pyramid of stones. His sons had fallen behind. No one spoke, for too much was at stake. In a little while they would know if all their hopes had been betrayed.

To east and west, the wall of mountains curved away as if embracing the land beneath. Below lay endless miles of undulating plain, with a great river swinging across it in tremendous loops. It was a fertile land; one in which the tribe could raise crops knowing that there would be no need to flee before the harvest came.

Then Shann lifted his eyes to the south, and saw the doom of all his hopes.

87

For there at the edge of the world glimmered that deadly light he had seen so often to the north – the glint of ice below the horizon.

There was no way forward. Through all the years of flight, the glaciers from the south had been advancing to meet them. Soon they would be crushed beneath the moving walls of ice ...

Southern glaciers did not reach the mountains until a generation later. In that last summer the sons of Shann carried the sacred treasures of the tribe to the lonely cairn overlooking the plain. The ice that had once gleamed below the horizon was now almost at their feet. By spring it would be splintering against the mountain walls.

No one understood the treasures now. They were from a past too distant for the understanding of any man alive. Their origins were lost in the mists that surrounded the Golden Age, and how they had come at last into the possession of this wandering tribe was a story that now would never be told. For it was the story of a civilization that had passed beyond recall.

Once, all these pitiful relics had been treasured for some good reason, and now they had become sacred though their meaning had long been lost. The print in the old books had faded centuries ago though much of the lettering was still visible – if there had been any to read it. But many generations had passed since anyone had had a use for a set of seven-figure logarithms, an atlas of the world, and the score of Sibelius' Seventh Symphony printed, according to the flyleaf, by H. K. Chu and Sons, at the City of Pekin in the year 2371 A.D.

The old books were placed reverently in the little crypt that had been made to receive them. There followed a motley collection of fragments – gold and platinum coins, a broken telephoto lens, a watch, a cold-light lamp, a microphone, the cutter from an electric razor, some midget radio tubes, the flotsam that had been left behind when the great tide of civilization had ebbed forever.

All these treasures were carefully stowed away in their resting place. Then came three more relics, the most sacred of all because the least understood.

The first was a strangely shaped piece of metal, showing the coloration of intense heat. It was, in its way, the most pathetic of all these symbols from the past, for it told of man's greatest achievement and of the future he might have known. The mahogany stand on which it was mounted bore a silver plate with the inscription:

Auxiliary Igniter from Starboard Jet
Spaceship "Morning Star"
Earth-Moon, A.D. 1985

Next followed another miracle of the ancient science – a sphere of transparent plastic with strangely shaped pieces of metal imbedded in it. At its center was a tiny capsule of synthetic radioelement, surrounded by the converting screens that shifted its radiation far down the spectrum. As long as the material remained active, the sphere would be a tiny radio transmitter, broadcasting power in all directions. Only a few of these spheres had ever been made. They had been designed as perpetual beacons to mark the orbits of the asteroids. But man had never reached the asteroids and the beacons had never been used.

Last of all was a flat, circular tin, wide in comparison with its depth. It was heavily sealed, and rattled when shaken. The tribal lore predicted that disaster would follow if it was ever opened, and no one knew that it held one of the great works of art of nearly a thousand years before.

The work was finished. The two men rolled the stones back into place and slowly began to descend the mountainside. Even to the last, man had given some thought to the future and had tried to preserve something for posterity.

That winter the great waves of ice began their first assault on the mountains, attacking from north and south. The foothills were overwhelmed in the first onslaught, and the glaciers ground them into dust. But the mountains stood firm, and when the summer came the ice retreated for a while.

So, winter after winter, the battle continued, and the roar of the avalanches, the grinding of rock and the explosions of splintering ice filled the air with tumult. No war of man's had been fiercer than this, and even man's battles had not quite engulfed the globe as this had done.

At last the tidal waves of ice began to subside and to creep slowly down the flanks of the mountains they had never quite subdued. The valleys and passes were still firmly in their grip. It was stalemate. The glaciers had met their match, but their defeat was too late to be of any use to man.

So the centuries passed, and presently there happened something that must occur once at least in the history of every world in the universe, no matter how remote and lonely it may be.

The ship from Venus came five thousand years too late, but its crew knew nothing of this. While still many millions of miles away, the telescopes had seen the great shroud of ice that made Earth the most brilliant object in the sky next to the sun itself.

Here and there the dazzling sheet was marred by black specks that revealed the presence of almost buried mountains. That was all. The rolling oceans, the plains and forests, the deserts and lakes – all that had been the world of man was sealed beneath the ice, perhaps forever.

The ship closed in to Earth and established an orbit less than a thousand miles away. For five days it circled the planet, while cameras recorded all that was left to see and a hundred instruments gathered information that would give the Venusian scientists many years of work.

An actual landing was not intended. There seemed little purpose in it. But on the sixth day the picture changed. A panoramic monitor, driven to the limit of its amplification, detected the dying radiation of the five-thousand-year-old beacon. Through all the centuries, it had been sending out its signals with ever-failing strength as its radioactive heart steadily weakened.

The monitor locked on the beacon frequency. In the control room, a bell clamored for attention. A little later, the Venusian ship broke free from its orbit and slanted down toward Earth, toward a range of mountains that still towered proudly above the ice, and to a cairn of gray stones that the years had scarcely touched. ...

The great disk of the sun blazed fiercely in a sky no longer veiled with mist, for the clouds that had once hidden Venus had now completely gone. Whatever force had caused the change in the sun's radiation had doomed one civilization, but had given birth to another. Less than five thousand years before, the half-savage people of Venus had seen sun and stars for the first time. Just as the science of Earth had begun with astronomy, so had that of Venus, and on the warm, rich world that man had never seen progress had been incredibly rapid.

Perhaps the Venusians had been lucky. They never knew the Dark Age that held man enchained for a thousand years. They missed the long detour into chemistry and mechanics but came at once to the more fundamental laws of radiation physics. In the time that man had taken to progress from the Pyramids to the rocket-propelled spaceship, the Venusians had passed from the discovery of agriculture to antigravity itself – the ultimate secret that man had never learned.

The warm ocean that still bore most of the young planet's life rolled its breakers languidly against the sandy shore. So new was this continent that the very sands were coarse and gritty. There had not yet been time enough for the sea to wear them smooth.

The scientists lay half in the water, their beautiful reptilian bodies gleaming in the sunlight. The greatest minds of Venus had gathered on this shore from all the islands of the planet. What they were going to hear they did not know, except that it concerned the Third World and the mysterious race that had peopled it before the coming of the ice.

The Historian was standing on the land, for the instruments he wished to use had no love of water. By his side was a large machine which attracted many curious glances from his colleagues. It was clearly concerned with optics, for a lens system projected from it toward a screen of white material a dozen yards away.

The Historian began to speak. Briefly he recapitulated what little had been discovered concerning the Third Planet and its people.

He mentioned the centuries of fruitless research that had failed to interpret a single word of the writings of Earth. The planet had been inhabited by a race of great technical ability. That, at least, was proved by the few pieces of machinery that had been found in the cairn upon the mountain.

"We do not know why so advanced a civilization came to an end," he observed. "Almost certainly, it had sufficient knowledge to survive an Ice Age. There must have been some other factor of which we know nothing. Possibly disease or racial degeneration may have been responsible. It has even been suggested that the tribal conflicts endemic to our own species in prehistoric times may have continued on the Third Planet after the coming of technology."

"Some philosophers maintain that knowledge of machinery does not necessarily imply a high degree of civilization, and it is theoretically possible to have wars in a society possessing mechanical power, flight, and even radio. Such a conception is alien to our thoughts, but we must admit its possibility. It would certainly account for the downfall of the lost race.

"It has always been assumed that we should never know anything of the physical form of the creatures who lived on Planet Three. For centuries our artists have been depicting scenes from the history of the dead world, peopling it with all manner of fantastic beings. Most of these creations have resembled us more or less closely, though it has often been pointed out that because *we* are reptiles it does not follow that all intelligent life must necessarily be reptilian.

"We now know the answer to one of the most baffling problems of history. At last, after hundreds of years of research, we have discovered the exact form and nature of the ruling life on the Third Planet."

There was a murmur of astonishment from the assembled scientists. Some were so taken aback that they disappeared for a while into the comfort of the ocean, as all Venusians were apt to do in moments of stress. The Historian waited until his colleagues re-emerged into the element they so disliked. He himself was quite comfortable, thanks to the tiny sprays that were continually playing over his body. With their help he could live on land for many hours before having to return to the ocean.

The excitement slowly subsided and the lecturer continued:

"One of the most puzzling of the objects found on Planet Three was a flat metal container holding a great length of transparent plastic material, perforated at the edges and wound tightly into a spool. This transparent tape at first seemed quite featureless, but an examination with the new subelectronic microscope has shown that this is not the case. Along the surface of the material, invisible to our eyes but perfectly clear under the correct radiation, are literally thousands of tiny pictures. It is believed that they were imprinted on the material by some chemical means, and have faded with the passage of time.

"These pictures apparently form a record of life as it was on the Third Planet at the height of its civilization. They are not independent. Consecutive pictures are almost identical, differing only in the detail of movement. The purpose of such a record is obvious. It is only necessary to project the scenes in rapid succession to give an illusion of continuous movement. We have made a machine to do this, and I have here an exact reproduction of the picture sequence.

"The scenes you are now going to witness take us back many thousands of years, to the great days of our sister planet. They show a complex civilization, many of whose activities we can only dimly understand. Life seems to have been very violent and energetic, and much that you will see is quite baffling.

"It is clear that the Third Planet was inhabited by a number of different species, none of them reptilian. That is a blow to our pride, but the conclusion is inescapable. The dominant type of life appears to have been a two-armed biped. It walked upright and covered its body with some flexible material, possibly for protection against the cold, since even before the Ice Age the planet was at a much lower temperature than our own world. But I will not try your patience any further. You will now see the record of which I have been speaking."

A brilliant light flashed from the projector. There was a gentle whirring, and on the screen appeared hundreds of strange beings moving rather jerkily to and fro. The picture expanded to embrace one of the creatures, and the scientists could see that the Historian's description had been correct.

The creature possessed two eyes, set rather close together, but the other facial adornments were a little obscure. There was a large orifice in the lower portion of the head that was continually opening and closing. Possibly it had something to do with the creature's breathing.

The scientists watched spellbound as the strange being became involved in a series of fantastic adventures. There was an incredibly violent conflict with another, slightly different creature. It seemed certain that they must both be killed, but when it was all over neither seemed any the worse.

Then came a furious drive over miles of country in a four-wheeled mechanical device which was capable of extraordinary feats of locomotion. The ride ended in a city packed with other vehicles moving in all directions at breathtaking speeds. No one was surprised to see two of the machines meet head-on with devastating results.

After that, events became even more complicated. It was now quite obvious that it would take many years of research to analyze and understand all that was happening. It was also clear that the record was a work of art, somewhat stylized, rather than an exact reproduction of life as it actually had been on the Third Planet.

Most of the scientists felt themselves completely dazed when the sequence of pictures came to an end. There was a final flurry of motion, in which the creature that had been the center of interest became involved in some tremendous but incomprehensible catastrophe. The picture contracted to a circle, centered on the creature's head.

The last scene of all was an expanded view of its face, obviously expressing some powerful emotion. But whether it was rage, grief, defiance, resignation or some other feeling could not be guessed. The picture vanished. For a moment some lettering appeared on the screen, then it was all over.

For several minutes there was complete silence, save for the lapping of the waves upon the sand. The scientists were too stunned to speak. The fleeting glimpse of Earth's civilization had had a shattering effect on their minds. Then little groups began to start talking together, first in whispers and then more and more loudly as the implications of what they had seen became clearer. Presently the Historian called for attention and addressed the meeting again.

"We are now planning," he said, "a vast program of research to extract all available knowledge from this record. Thousands of copies are being made for distribution to all workers. You will appreciate the problems involved. The psychologists in particular have an immense task confronting them.

"But I do not doubt that we shall succeed. In another generation, who can say what we may not have learned of this wonderful race? Before we leave, let us look again at our remote cousins, whose wisdom may have surpassed our own but of whom so little has survived."

Once more the final picture flashed on the screen, motionless this time, for the projector had been stopped. With something like awe, the scientists gazed at the still figure from the past, while in turn the little biped stared back at them with its characteristic expression of arrogant bad temper.

For the rest of time it would symbolize the human race. The psychologists of Venus would analyze its actions and watch its every movement until they could reconstruct its mind. Thousands of books would be written about it. Intricate philosophies would be contrived to account for its behavior.

But all this labor, all this research, would be utterly in vain. Perhaps the proud and lonely figure on the screen was smiling sardonically at the scientists who were starting on their age-long fruitless quest.

Its secret would be safe as long as the universe endured, for no one now would ever read the lost language of Earth. Millions of times in the ages to come those last few words would flash across the screen, and none could ever guess their meaning:

A Walt Disney Production.

Biographical Notes

Arthur C. Clarke was born in Somerset in 1917. He took a science degree at London University with first-class honours. During the Second World War he was an RAF officer, and responsible for experimental radar equipment. In 1945 he published a technical paper on the principles of satellite communication. While working as an editor of a science magazine he also began writing science fiction. In this field he soon acquired an enormous reputation, and has been compared with Jules Verne and H.G. Wells. He has won numerous prizes both for his fiction and his "serious" science writing.

Clarke, History Lesson

Among his over forty books one must mention the non-fiction (but highly speculative) works The Exploration of Space *(1951) and* Profiles of the Future *(1962). The story we have included here is from his collection* Across the Sea of Stars *(1959). His other works of fiction include* Childhood's End, Earthlight *and* A Fall of Moondust. *He also wrote the screenplay (with Stanley Kubrick) for the film.* 2001: A Space Odyssey.

Arthur C. Clarke is now living in Sri Lanka, where he is Chancellor of a university.

Annotations

53	10	glacier [ˈglæsjə, ˈgleɪʃə]	river of ice
	11	to kindle	to light
	12	remorseless	merciless, not stopping for anything
		to batter	to beat
		in vain	without success
	13	refuge [ˈrefjuːdʒ]	safety, a safe place
	19	to wane	to come to an end, to fade away
	22	cairn [keən]	a pile of stones
	26	**at stake**	at risk
	28	**to embrace**	to put one's arms around
	29	to undulate	to go up and down in gentle waves
	33	**doom**	ruin, end of all hope
54	15	to pass beyond recall	to be totally forgotten
	17	**sacred** [ˈseɪkrəd]	holy
	18	**to fade**	to lose colour
	21	score	written notes of a symphony
	22	flyleaf	an otherwise empty page at the beginning of a book
	24	**reverently**	with great respect
		crypt	underground chamber
	25	motley	very mixed
	27	midget	miniature
		flotsam	things washed up on a beach
	28	**to ebb**	(of the tide, or a flood) to go down
	29	to stow away	to put in storage
	36	auxiliary	additional, supporting
		igniter [ɪgˈnaɪtə]	s.th. used to start an engine
		starboard	(on a ship) right-hand
55	1	sphere	solid round object
	7	**perpetual**	everlasting
		beacon [ˈbiːkən]	s.th. which sends out signals (usually light)
		orbit	path (of a planet, etc.)
	11	lore	(also "folklore") traditional wisdom, stories, etc.
	16	**posterity**	future generations

Clarke, History Lesson

	17	assault, onslaught	attack
	21	avalanche ['ævəlɑːnʃ]	mass of snow and rock gliding down a mountain
	24	to engulf	to swallow up, to cover completely
	25	to subside	(of water, ice, etc.) to go down again
	26	**to subdue**	to conquer
	27	stalemate	a situation where neither side can win
		to meet one's match	to come across an equally strong opponent
	31	**remote**	far away
	34	shroud	white covering (for a dead body)
	36	to mar	to spoil the beauty of
56	7	amplification	(electronic) strengthening of a signal
	9	ever-failing	getting weaker all the time
	11	to clamor [æ]	to make a loud demand
	15	**to veil** [eɪ]	to cover (usually with a light cloth)
	19	**savage** ['sævɪdʒ]	wild, uncivilized
	24	detour	indirect way
	28	**gravity** ['grævɪtɪ]	the force that attracts us to the earth
	31	breakers	waves
		languid	lazy
57	6	fruitless research	studies that have no useful results
	14	endemic [–'– –]	widespread
	20	**alien** ['eɪljən]	foreign, strange
	29	baffling	puzzling
	33	taken aback	astonished and disturbed
	34	to be apt to	to tend to
58	2	spool	a roll (of string, tape, etc.)
	3	featureless	with nothing on it
	10	**consecutive** [–'– – –]	in a sequence, one after the other
	24	biped ['baɪped]	two-legged creature
	27	to try (s.o.'s patience)	to put under pressure, to test
	29	whirring	sound made by s.th. turning
	30	jerkily	with sudden short movements
	31	to and fro	backwards and forwards
	34	adornment	decoration, feature
		obscure	not clear
		orifice	opening in the body
	37	spellbound	fascinated
59	2	feat	achievement
		locomotion	movement from one place to another
	5	devastating	terribly destructive
	11	dazed, stunned	dizzy and confused, as if hit on the head
	12	flurry	sudden burst of activity
	13	**tremendous**	enormous; terrible
	17	**defiance**	resistance; provocative behaviour
	21	fleeting glimpse	very short look at s.th.
	22	**shattering**	deeply disturbing
	29	**to appreciate**	to understand
	33	**to surpass**	to go beyond, to exceed

	36	**awe**	great respect
60	2	intricate ['ɪntrɪkət]	complicated
		to contrive	to fabricate
		to account for	to explain
	4	sardonic	mocking
	5	**quest**	search
	6	to endure	to last

Interpretation and Teaching Notes

Background, Content and Analysis

Science fiction is full of surprises. This fact in itself could have justified the inclusion of almost any Arthur C. Clarke story in our anthology. Our choice of "History Lesson" in particular has to do with its classic surprise ending, which, for once, is a light-hearted one – or is there a touch of pathos behind it?

Even if one can discover a certain seriousness of intent in the story, it is basically a joke, and leafing through to the end could certainly spoil it. It was, in fact, spoiled for its original readers: the magazine which first published it added an illustration which gave away the whole point[1]. Shame on them!

(The assumption from here on is that anyone who hasn't yet read the story and doesn't want the ending given away has no business reading these notes.)

The story covers the decline of one planetary civilization and the rise of another, and involves the lapse of something over five thousand years. But the galactic perspective makes this shrink to almost nothing. Three scenes are all it takes to make the point.

The first two of these take place on earth. In the first scene we see a human tribe fleeing southward from the encroaching ice. It seems to be a primitive tribe, travelling on foot with their animals, camping wherever they see a chance of growing the crops they need to survive (**53** 8, 15–16, 30–32). They seem to have no knowledge of their history, except for vague memories and legends (**53** 1–3, 13).

But far from belonging in the distant past of the human race, they are – from our point of view – its future. An ice age of such a devastating nature has not yet happened on our earth (and it is our earth, as will be confirmed on the next page). What Shann, the leader of the tribe, realizes to his dismay from his vantage point on the mountain (**53** 33–**54** 5), is that the glaciers spreading from both poles are about to meet at the equator.

They are, therefore, the degenerated and pathetic remains of life on earth. This is confirmed in the second scene (**54** 6–**55** 31), where we see the "sons of Shann", the next and last generation, reverently burying the relics they have been carrying around with them on their wanderings. Their respect for these relics is not based on any understanding of them, whether

---

[1] The "unspeakable" illustration is referred to in: Damon Knight, *A Sense of Wonder, Essays on Modern Science Fiction,* Chicago: Advent Publishers, 1967.

they tell of a great technical or artistic achievement. It is purely of a superstitious nature, like the taboo surrounding the "great work of art" in a tin (**55** 10–13) which is to play such an important part in the stoy.

Altogether, these relics hint at a possible (future) history of our race which retains a certain plausibility, even if a few details would have to be changed to take account of actual events since the story was written[2]. It seems there has been further technological progress (**55** 1–9), and considerable political change. China seems to have become the dominant power, with its capital a major centre of world culture (**54** 21–23). We are not, however, told the cause of the ultimate decline of the human race. Like the Venusians, we can only speculate.

Having done what they can to "preserve something for posterity", the last representatives of humanity go down from the mountain. Man disappears from the scene and the battle of the glaciers takes over. The burial of the relics seems to have been a vain and superstitious gesture.

Meanwhile, back on Venus, and only a couple of thousand years later ... The third and longest section, for which the first two have been necessary preludes, is set on our neighbouring planet. Conditions there have changed as drastically as those on earth, but here they have allowed for the rapid rise of intelligent life and the development of a technology even surpassing what man had achieved (**56** 23–29).

One of its spaceships finally lands on earth, having been attracted by the perpetual radioactive beacon that had been buried with the rest of the treasures of the tribe of Shann. What they find under the cairn of stone provides their scientists with an undreamed-of chance to find out something about life on the dead planet.

That these scientists are reptiles is one of the charms of the story. The picture of them basking on the shore as they listen to the Historian's lecture (**56** 34–40, **57** 32–38) is likely to tickle any Earthling's sense of humour. Of course we know that just because we are mammals, it does not follow that all intelligent life must necessarily be mammalian, but ... – the anthropocentric prejudice that gives rise to visions of little green men, etc. is nicely parodied by one of the Historian's introductory remarks (**57** 25–28).

Another barb aimed at mankind is implicit in his difficulty in envisioning a technologically advanced society in which tribal conflicts still continue – this would, of course, explain their downfall (**57** 10–21).

---

[2] Clarke has been unnecessarily cautious in putting the first moon landing as late as 1985. Three years later, in *Profiles of the Future,* his prediction is a more accurate 1970. Or is he referring in a general way to space travel or routine moon landings as "man's greatest achievement" (**54** 33)? The other detail one would change if writing today would be the spelling of the capital of China, now officially "Beijing".

Apart from such satirical side-swipes, the main function of this long-winded preamble – the lecture takes up nearly half the total length of the story – is to generate suspense, in the form of curiosity as to what on Earth or Venus they have found out about us. And the Historian is confident that they have, indeed, discovered "the exact form and nature of the ruling life on the Third Planet" (**57** 31).

They have not been able to decipher any of the writings of Earth, but one of the treasures is apparently more informative than any book. The "work of art" in the round tin box is of course a film, and they have found out how it works. More suspense as the Historian laboriously sums up his findings, and even more as the Venusians watch the fantastic adventures and violent conflicts (**58** 38) of the film.

Only in the very final line of the story is it (indirectly) revealed (though some clever readers may have begun to guess) that the "two-armed biped" (**58** 23–24) with its "characteristic expression of arrogant bad temper" (**59** 38) who will "for the rest of time ... symbolize the human race" (**59** 39) can be none other than Donald Duck.

Well, the joke is on the Venusians – and, of course, on those readers who didn't guess before the ending. But there is a sense in which the joke may be on all of us, as a race.

What if after the natural decline or self-inflicted destruction of the human race no memory were to remain of us but Donald Duck? The galactic perspective may make us seem very small indeed and our petty concerns (and "tribal conflicts") trivial, but not the question of whether it matters. The pathos permeating the author's treatment (**54** 16ff) of the "pitiful relics" of human civilization suggest at least a certain sadness at the thought[3].

On the other hand, any memory may be better than none. And the impression the Venusians get of us from the aggressive antics of Donald Duck may not be too far off the mark.

One of the more important effects of good science fiction is that it forces us into a consideration of the previously unthought and seemingly unthinkable. And here we have it as a result of one of the author's more lightweight works.

---

[3] In his *Profiles of the Future* (London 1962; pp. 215–6, Penguin edition, 1964) Arthur C. Clarke explicitly rejects such sadness at the probable extinction of the human race. Reacting to those who find it a "bleak prospect" he says, "This ... is an attitude I find impossible to share. No individual lives forever; why should we expect our species to be immortal?" He is referring here, however, to our possible replacement by machines.

Recommended Teaching Units (Overview)

I. Classroom reading of first section, to **55** 31 (but only cursory reading of passage **54** 16–**55** 13); discussion of content (end of the human race, burying of the treasures).

II. Home study of passage describing the treasures (**54** 16–**55** 13), discussion of what they reveal; classroom reading up to **55** 38 (Venusian scientists' convention, announcement of breakthrough in their study of the lost race) or **58** 15 (announcement of the film).

III. Home reading of end of story; discussion of the joke.

Unit I
Last of the Race

Note: If a double period is available, the homework suggested here can alternatively be dealt with in class (see point 4.).

1. Lines **53** 1–14
After reading each of these three paragraphs silently (and dealing with any vocabulary difficulties), the students can be asked to consider how much they now know about the setting of the story – and possibly more important – what they still don't know.
Paragraph 1: A wandering tribe (Where? When?).
Paragraph 2: Ice Age (Which?/When?).
Paragraph 3: Legends – hints of a past culture (What? When?). The students should be encouraged to use their knowledge of palaeontology, geology and prehistory in deciding whether this could be in the distant past of the human race. Those who know Arthur C. Clarke to be a writer of science fiction will consider whether the setting could even be a different planet.

2. Lines **53** 15–**54** 5
Again, silent reading is recommended, to be followed by a series of comprehension questions:
Why did Shann go ahead of the tribe?
Why was he trembling as he neared the top of the mountain?
What good thing did he see?
What bad thing did he see?

3. Lines **54** 6–15
For variety and dramatic effect we recommend that these lines (and later also **55** 14–31, i.e. the beginning and end of this section of the story) be read aloud by the teacher.

How much time has now elapsed?
Why should the "sons of Shann" wish to bury these "treasures"?
Do you now think you know what historical age this is?

4. Lines **54** 16–**55** 13 (the treasures)
Unless the time is available to discuss this passage in detail, the students should here be merely given the opportunity to skim these paragraphs silently to get a rough impression of the nature of the "treasures", and to grasp that they include relics of our own time.
Can you say now what historical period Shann belongs to?

5. Lines **55** 14–31 to be read aloud.

Homework: Re-read the passage dealing with the treasures. When you have understood everything, write in a few sentences what they tell you about the "past" – in other words, a "Short History of the Human Race".

Unit II
Meanwhile, Back on Venus ...

1. The rise and fall of human civilization
A number of students should be asked to read their "Short Histories" aloud, for comparison and discussion.

2. Meaning of last sentence of section (**55** 29–31)
What is the author suggesting "must occur once at least in the history of every world in the universe"?
Do you agree that it must occur?

3. Lines **55** 32–**56** 14 (the landing)
The first paragraph (or maybe the first two) of this section should best be read aloud – otherwise silent reading, to be followed by comprehension questions.
We now have a new point of view – what is it?
What is most noticeable about the Earth?
How – and why – do the Venusians approach it?
Why do they change their plans and land?

4. Lines **56** 15–33 (Venusian history)
Silent reading followed by comprehension questions.
What information is given in this passage?
When did life emerge on Venus?
Sum up the history of the Venusians.
How did it differ from that of the human race?

5. Lines **56** 34–**57** 38 (the scientists' convention)
Again, silent reading is recommended.
What kind of creatures are the Venusians? / What is surprising about the Venusians?
What group of them have gathered together – and why?
Who addresses the meeting?
What is the meeting about?
What problems does the speaker mention?
What startling news does he have for his listeners?
How do they react?

6. Speculation
How do you think they have found out about the nature of life on Earth?
Which of the "treasures" do you think was most useful to them?
If enough time is available, the class should now read – or have read to them – the next two paragraphs (**57** 39–**58** 15: the revelation that one of the treasures is in fact a film).
Otherwise this passage can also be left for private reading at home.

Homework: Finish the story.

Unit III
Man: The Movie

1. Comprehension
What movie have the Venusians been watching?
How do you know?
There may be some dispute as to which Walt Disney character is actually referred to, but this does not matter as long as the students can quote the relevant descriptions in support of their opinion.

2. Effect of the ending (discussion)
How did you react when you read the ending?
Had you begun to guess what kind of movie it was?
– At what point did you begin to guess?
– What other kind of movie did you think it was?
How did the author keep up the suspense?
It should be noted here that our sharing of the Venusians' point of view serves to uphold the suspense in two ways – we share their excitement at the build-up to this "historic" moment, and we share their ignorance. In addition, we naturally want to know by what movie we will be remembered for all time!